WEST SIDE STORY

West Side Story

A Musical

(Based on a conception of Jerome Robbins)

Book by
Arthur Laurents

Music by
Leonard Bernstein

Lyrics by
Stephen Sondheim

Entire production directed and choreographed by
Jerome Robbins

RANDOM HOUSE
NEW YORK

THIRTEENTH PRINTING, MAY 1969

G. Shirmer, Inc., and Chappell & Co., Inc., are publishers of the music of WEST SIDE STORY

Photographs by courtesy of Fred Fehl

Library of Congress Catalog Card Number: 58–6982

MANUFACTURED IN THE UNITED STATES OF AMERICA

WEST SIDE STORY *was first presented by Robert E. Griffith and Harold S. Prince, by arrangement with Roger L. Stevens, at the Winter Garden, New York City, September 26, 1957, with the following cast:*

THE JETS

RIFF (The Leader)	Mickey Calin
TONY (His Friend)	Larry Kert
ACTION	Eddie Roll
A-RAB	Tony Mordente
BABY JOHN	David Winters
SNOWBOY	Grover Dale
BIG DEAL	Martin Charnin
DIESEL	Hank Brunjes
GEE-TAR	Tommy Abbott
MOUTHPIECE	Frank Green
TIGER	Lowell Harris

THEIR GIRLS

GRAZIELLA	Wilma Curley
VELMA	Carole D'Andrea
MINNIE	Nanette Rosen
CLARICE	Marilyn D'Honau
PAULINE	Julie Oser
ANYBODYS	Lee Becker

THE SHARKS

BERNARDO (The Leader)	Ken Le Roy
MARIA (His Sister)	Carol Lawrence
ANITA (His Girl)	Chita Rivera
CHINO (His Friend)	Jamie Sanchez
PEPE	George Marcy
INDIO	Noel Schwartz

LUIS	Al De Sio
ANXIOUS	Gene Gavin
NIBBLES	Ronnie Lee
JUANO	Jay Norman
TORO	Erne Castaldo
MOOSE	Jack Murray

THEIR GIRLS

ROSALIA	Marilyn Cooper
CONSUELO	Reri Grist
TERESITA	Carmen Guiterrez
FRANCISCA	Elizabeth Taylor
ESTELLA	Lynn Ross
MARGARITA	Liane Plane

THE ADULTS

DOC	Art Smith
SCHRANK	Arch Johnson
KRUPKE	William Bramley
GLAD HAND	John Harkins

Entire production directed and choreographed by Jerome Robbins

Scenic production by Oliver Smith

Costumes designed by Irene Sharaff

Lighting by Jean Rosenthal

Musical direction by Max Goberman

Orchestrations by Leonard Bernstein, *with* Sid Ramin *and* Irwin Kostal

Co-choreographer: Peter Gennaro

Production Associate: Sylvia Drulie

The action takes place on the West Side of New York City during the last days of summer.

Act One

PROLOGUE: THE MONTHS BEFORE

5:00 P.M.	The Street
5:30 P.M.	A Back Yard
6:00 P.M.	A Bridal Shop
10:00 P.M.	The Gym
11:00 P.M.	A Back Alley
MIDNIGHT	The Drugstore

THE NEXT DAY

5:30 P.M.	The Bridal Shop
6:00 to 9:00 P.M.	The Neighborhood
9:00 P.M.	Under the Highway

Act Two

9:15 P.M.	A Bedroom
10:00 P.M.	Another Alley
11:30 P.M.	The Bedroom
11:40 P.M.	The Drugstore
11:50 P.M.	The Cellar
MIDNIGHT	The Street

MUSICAL NUMBERS

ACT ONE

PROLOGUE	Danced by Jets and Sharks
JET SONG	Riff and Jets
"SOMETHING'S COMING"	Tony
THE DANCE AT THE GYM	Jets and Sharks
"MARIA"	Tony
"TONIGHT"	Tony and Maria
"AMERICA"	Anita, Rosalia, and Shark Girls
"COOL"	Riff and the Jets
"ONE HAND, ONE HEART"	Tony and Maria
"TONIGHT" (Quintet and Chorus)	Company
THE RUMBLE	Riff, Bernardo, Jets and Sharks

ACT TWO

"I FEEL PRETTY"	Maria, Rosalia, Teresita, Francisca
"SOMEWHERE"	Danced by Company; Sung by Consuelo
"GEE, OFFICER KRUPKE"	Action, Snowboy, and Jets
"A BOY LIKE THAT"	Anita and Maria
"I HAVE A LOVE"	Anita and Maria
TAUNTING	Anita and the Jets
FINALE	Company

ACT ONE

ACT ONE

Scene I

5:00 P.M. *The street.*

A suggestion of city streets and alleyways; a brick wall.

The opening is musical: half-danced, half-mimed, with occasional phrases of dialogue. It is primarily a condensation of the growing rivalry between two teen-age gangs, the Jets and the Sharks, each of which has its own prideful uniform. The boys—sideburned, long-haired—are vital, restless, sardonic; the Sharks are Puerto Ricans, the Jets an anthology of what is called American.

The action begins with the Jets in possession of the area: owning, enjoying, loving their "home." Their leader is RIFF: *glowing, driving, intelligent, slightly whacky. His lieutenant is* DIESEL: *big, slow, steady, nice. The youngest member of the gang is* BABY JOHN: *awed at everything, including that he is a Jet, trying to act the big man. His buddy is* A-RAB: *an explosive little ferret who enjoys everything and understands the seriousness of nothing. The most aggressive is* ACTION: *a catlike ball of fury. We will get to know these boys better later, as well as* SNOWBOY: *a bespectacled self-styled expert.*

The first interruption of the Jets' sunny mood is the sharply punctuated entrance of the leader of the Sharks, BERNARDO: *handsome, proud, fluid, a chip on his sardonic shoulder. The Jets, by far in the majority, flick him off. He returns with other Sharks: they, too, are flicked off. But the numerical supremacy, the strength of the Jets, is gradually being threatened. The be-*

ginnings of warfare are mild at first: a boy being tripped up, or being sandbagged with a flour sack or even being spit on—all with overly elaborate apologies.

Finally, A-RAB *comes across the suddenly deserted area, pretending to be an airplane. There is no sound as he zooms along in fancied flight. Then over the wall drops* BERNARDO. *Another Shark, another and another appear, blocking* A-RAB'S *panicky efforts at escape. They close in, grab him, pummel him, as a Shark on top of the wall is stationed as lookout. Finally,* BERNARDO *bends over* A-RAB *and makes a gesture (piercing his ear); the lookout whistles; Jets tear on, Sharks tear on, and a free-for-all breaks out.* RIFF *goes at once to* A-RAB, *like a protective father. The fight is stopped by a police whistle, louder and louder, and the arrival of a big goonlike cop,* KRUPKE, *and a plain-clothes man,* SCHRANK. SCHRANK *is strong, always in command; he has a charming, pleasant manner, which he often employs to cover his venom and his fear.*

KRUPKE

Knock it off! Settle down.

SCHRANK

All right: *kill each other!* . . . But not on my beat.

RIFF

(*Such innocence*)

Why if it isn't Lieutenant Schrank!

SEVERAL JETS

(*Dancing-class manners*)

Top of the day, Lieutenant Schrank.

BERNARDO

(*One with Riff*)

And Officer Krupke!

SEVERAL SHARKS

Top of the day, Officer Krupke.

SCHRANK

Boy, what you Puerto Ricans have done to this neighborhood. Which one of 'em clobbered ya, A-rab?

(A-RAB *looks to* RIFF, *who takes over with great helpful seriousness.*)

RIFF

As a matter of factuality, sir, we suspicion the job was done by a cop.

SNOWBOY

Two cops.

A-RAB

Oh, at least!

KRUPKE

Impossible!

SCHRANK

Didn't nobody tell ya there's a difference between bein' a stool pigeon and co-operatin' with the law?

RIFF

You told us the difference, sir. And we all chipped in for a prize for the first guy who can figure it out.

ACTION

(*Indicating* SCHRANK)

Maybe buddy boy should get the prize.

SCHRANK

Don't buddy boy me, Action! I got a hot surprise for you: you hoodlums don't own the streets. There's been too much raiding between you and the PRs. All right, Bernardo, get your trash outa here. (*Mock charm*) Please.

BERNARDO

Let's go, Sharks.

(*They exit.*)

SCHRANK

(*To the* JETS)

If I don't put down the roughhouse, I get put down—on a traffic corner. Your friend don't like traffic corners. So you buddy boys are gonna play ball with me. I gotta put up with them and so do you. *You're gonna make nice with them PRs from now on.* Because otherwise I'm gonna beat the crap outa every one of ya and *then* run ya in. Say good-bye to the nice boys, Krupke.

KRUPKE

Good-bye, boys.

(*He follows* SCHRANK *out.*)

SNOWBOY

(*Imitating* KRUPKE)

Good-bye, boys.

A-RAB

They make a very nice couple.

ACTION

(*Bitterly*)

"You hoodlums don't own the streets."

SNOWBOY

Go play in the park!

ACTION

Keep off the grass!

BABY JOHN

Get outa the house!

ACTION

Keep off the block!

A-RAB

Get outa *here!*

ACTION

Keep off the world! A gang that don't own a street is nuthin'!

RIFF

WE DO OWN IT! Jets—square off! Acemen: (DIESEL, ACTION *and* SNOWBOY *line up at attention*) Rocketmen: (*Three others line up*) Rank-and-file:

(*Sheepishly,* A-RAB *trudges into position,* BABY JOHN *behind him.*)

BABY JOHN

(*Shocked, to* A-RAB)

Gee, your ear's got blood on it!

A-RAB

(*Proudly*)

I'm a casual, Baby John.

BABY JOHN

(*Examining the ear*)

Them PRs! They branded you!

SNOWBOY

That makes you a Puerto Rican tomato. Cha-cha-cha señorita?

RIFF

Cut the frabbajabba. Which one of the Sharks did it?

A-RAB

Bernardo. 'Cause I heard him say: "Thees ees for stink, bombin' my old man's store."

(*He makes the same gesture* BERNARDO *made when he pierced his ear.*)

BABY JOHN

Ouch!

ACTION

You shoulda done worse. Them PRs're the reason my old man's gone bust.

RIFF

Who says?

ACTION

My old man says.

BABY JOHN

(*To* A-RAB)

My old man says his old man woulda gone bust anyway.

ACTION

Your old man says what?

BABY JOHN

My old man says them Puerto Ricans is ruinin' free ennaprise.

ACTION

And what're we doin' about it?

(Pushing through the gang comes a scrawny teen-age girl, dressed in an outfit that is a pathetic attempt to imitate that of the Jets. Perhaps we have glimpsed her in the fracas before the police came in. Her name is ANYBODYS.*)*

ANYBODYS

Gassin', crabbin'—

ACTION

You still around?

ANYBODYS

Listen, I was a smash in that fight. Oh, Riff, Riff, I was murder!

RIFF

Come on, Anybodys—

ANYBODYS

Riff, how about me gettin' in the gang now?

A-RAB

How about the gang gettin' in—ahhh, who'd wanta!

ANYBODYS

You cheap beast!

(*She lunges for* A-RAB, *but* RIFF *pulls her off and pushes her out.*)

RIFF

The road, little lady, the road. (*In a moment of bravado, just before she goes,* ANYBODYS *spits—but cautiously*) Round out! (*This is* RIFF'S *summoning of the gang, and they surround him*) We fought hard for this territory and it's ours. But with those cops servin' as cover, the PRs can move in right under our noses and take it away. *Unless* we speed fast and clean 'em up in one all-out fight!

ACTION

(*Eagerly*)

A rumble! (*A jabbing gesture*) Chung! Chung!

RIFF

Cool, Action boy. The Sharks want a place, too, and *they are tough*. They might ask for bottles or knives or zip guns.

BABY JOHN

Zip guns . . . Gee!

RIFF

I'm not finalizin' and sayin' they will: I'm only sayin' they might and we gotta be prepared. Now, what's your mood?

ACTION

I say go, go!!

SNOWBOY

But if they say knives or guns—

BABY JOHN

I say let's forget the whole thing.

DIESEL

What do you say, Riff?

RIFF

I say this turf is small, *but it's all we got.* I wanna hold it like we always held it: with skin! But if they say switchblades, I'll get a switchblade. I say I want the Jets to be Number One, to sail, to hold the sky!

DIESEL

Then rev us off. (*A punching gesture*) Voom-va voom!

ACTION

Chung chung!

A-RAB

Cracko, jacko!

SNOWBOY

Riga diga dum!

BABY JOHN

Pam pam!!

RIFF

O.K., buddy boys, we rumble! (*General glee*) Now protocality calls for a war council to decide on weapons. I'll make the challenge to Bernardo.

SNOWBOY

You gotta take a lieutenant.

ACTION

That's me!

RIFF

That's Tony.

ACTION

Who needs Tony?
(*Music starts.*)

RIFF

Against the Sharks we need every man we got.

ACTION

Tony don't belong any more.

RIFF

Cut it, Action boy. I and Tony started the Jets.

ACTION

Well, he acts like he don't wanna belong.

BABY JOHN

Who wouldn't wanna belong to the Jets!

ACTION

Tony ain't been with us for over a month.

SNOWBOY

What about the day we clobbered the Emeralds?

A-RAB

Which we couldn't have done without Tony.

BABY JOHN

He saved my ever lovin' neck.

RIFF

Right. He's always come through for us and he will now.
(He sings)
When you're a Jet,
You're a Jet all the way
From your first cigarette
To your last dyin' day.
When you're a Jet,
If the spit hits the fan,
You got brothers around,
You're a family man!
You're never alone,
You're never disconnected!
You're home with your own—
When company's expected,
You're well protected!
Then you are set
With a capital J,
Which you'll never forget
Till they cart you away.
When you're a Jet,
You stay
A jet!
(He speaks)
I know Tony like I know me. I guarantee you can count him in.

ACTION

In, out, let's get crackin'.

A-RAB

Where you gonna find Bernardo?

RIFF

At the dance tonight at the gym.

BIG DEAL

But the gym's neutral territory.

RIFF

(*Sweet innocence*)

I'm gonna make nice there! I'm only gonna challenge him.

A-RAB

Great, Daddy-O!

RIFF

So everybody dress up sweet and sharp. Meet Tony and me at ten. And walk tall!

(*He runs off.*)

A-RAB

We always walk tall!

BABY JOHN

We're Jets!

ACTION

The greatest!

(*He sings with* BABY JOHN)

When you're a Jet,
You're the top cat in town,

You're the gold-medal kid
With the heavyweight crown!

(A-RAB, ACTION, BIG DEAL *sing*)

When you're a Jet,
You're the swingin'est thing.
Little boy, you're a man;
Little boy, you're a king!

(ALL)

The Jets are in gear,
Our cylinders are clickin'!
The Sharks'll steer clear
'Cause every Puerto Rican
'S a lousy chicken!

Here come the Jets
Like a bat out of hell—
Someone gets in our way,
Someone don't feel so well!
Here come the Jets:
Little world, step aside!
Better go underground,
Better run, better hide!
We're drawin' the line,
So keep your noses hidden!
We're hangin' a sign
Says "Visitors forbidden"—
And we ain't kiddin'!
Here come the Jets,
Yeah! And we're gonna beat
Every last buggin' gang
On the whole buggin' street!

(DIESEL *and* ACTION)
On the whole!

(ALL)
Ever—!
Mother—!
Lovin'—!
Street!

The Lights Black Out

Scene 2

5:30 P.M. *A back yard.*

On a small ladder, a good-looking sandy-haired boy is painting a vertical sign that will say: Doc's. Below, RIFF *is haranguing.*

RIFF

Riga tiga tum tum. Why not? . . . You can't say ya won't, Tony boy, without sayin' why not?

TONY

(*Grins*)

Why not?

RIFF

Because it's me askin': Riff. Womb to tomb!

TONY

Sperm to worm! (*Surveying the sign*) You sure this looks like skywritin'?

RIFF

It's brilliant.

TONY

Twenty-seven years the boss has had that drugstore. I wanna surprise him with a new sign.

RIFF

(*Shaking the ladder*)

Tony, this is important!

TONY

Very important: Acemen, Rocketmen.

RIFF

What's with you? Four and one-half years I live with a buddy and his family. Four and one-half years I think I know a man's character. Buddy boy, I am a victim of disappointment in you.

TONY

End your sufferin', little man. Why don't you pack up your gear and clear out?

RIFF

'Cause your ma's hot for me. (TONY *grabs his arm and twists it*) No! 'Cause I hate livin' with my buggin' uncle uncle UNCLE!

(TONY *releases him and climbs back up the ladder.*)

TONY

Now go play nice with the Jets.

RIFF

The Jets are the greatest!

TONY

Were.

RIFF

Are. You found somethin' better?

TONY

No. But—

RIFF

But what?

TONY

You won't dig it.

RIFF

Try me.

TONY

O.K. . . . Every single damn night for the last month, I wake up—and I'm reachin' out.

RIFF

For what?

TONY

I don't know. It's right outside the door, around the corner. But it's comin'!

RIFF

What is? Tell me!

TONY

I don't know! It's—like the kick I used to get from bein' a Jet.

RIFF

(*Quietly*)

. . . Or from bein' buddies.

TONY

We're still buddies.

RIFF

The kick comes from people, buddy boy.

TONY

Yeah, but not from being a Jet.

RIFF

No? Without a gang you're an orphan. With a gang you walk in two's, three's, four's. And when your gang is the best, when you're a Jet, buddy boy, you're out in the sun and home free home!

TONY

Riff, I've had it.

(*Pause.*)

RIFF

Tony, the trouble is large: the Sharks bite hard! We got to stop them now, and we need *you!* (*Pause. Quietly*) I never asked the time of day from a clock, but I'm askin' you: Come to the dance tonight . . . (TONY *turns away*) . . . I already told the gang you'd be there.

TONY

(*After a moment, turns to him with a grin*)

What time?

RIFF

Ten?

TONY

Ten it is.

RIFF

Womb to tomb!

TONY

Sperm to worm! And I'll live to regret this.

RIFF

Who knows? Maybe what you're waitin' for'll be twitchin' at the dance!

(He runs off.)

TONY

Who knows?
(Music starts and he sings)
Could be! . . .
Who knows? . . .
There's something due any day;
I will know right away
Soon as it shows.
It may come cannonballin' down through the sky,
Gleam in its eye,
Bright as a rose!
Who knows? . . .
It's only just out of reach,
Down the block, on a beach,
Under a tree.
I got a feeling there's a miracle due,
Gonna come true,
Coming to me!

Could it be? Yes, it could.
Something's coming, something good,
If I can wait!
Something's coming, I don't know what it is
But it is
Gonna be great!

With a click, with a shock,

Phone'll jingle, door'll knock,
Open the latch!
Something's coming, don't know when, but it's soon—
Catch the moon,
One-handed catch!

Around the corner,
Or whistling down the river,
Come on—deliver
To me!

Will it be? Yes, it will.
Maybe just by holding still
It'll be there!
Come on, something, come on in, don't be shy,
Meet a guy,
Pull up a chair!

The air is humming,
And something great is coming!
Who knows?
It's only just out of reach,
Down the block, on a beach . . .
Maybe tonight . . .

The Lights Dim

Scene 3

6:00 P.M. *A bridal shop.*

A small section, enough to include a table with sewing machine, a chair or two.

ANITA, *a Puerto Rican girl with loose hair and slightly flashy clothes, is finishing remaking what was a white communion dress into a party dress for an extremely lovely, extremely young girl:* MARIA. ANITA *is knowing, sexual, sharp.* MARIA *is an excited, enthusiastic, obedient child, with the temper, stubborn strength and awareness of a woman.*

MARIA

(*Holding out scissors*)

Por favor, Anita. Make the neck lower!

ANITA

Stop it, Maria.

MARIA

One inch. How much can one little inch do?

ANITA

Too much.

MARIA

(*Exasperated*)

Anita, it is now to be a dress for dancing, no longer for kneeling in front of an altar.

ANITA

With those boys you can start in dancing and end up kneeling.

MARIA

Querida, one little inch; *una poca poca*—

ANITA

Bernardo made me promise—

MARIA

Ai! Bernardo! One month have I been in this country—do I ever even touch excitement? I sew all day, I sit all night. For what did my fine brother bring me here?

ANITA

To marry Chino.

MARIA

When I look at Chino, nothing happens.

ANITA

What do you expect to happen?

MARIA

I don't know: something. What happens when you look at Bernardo?

ANITA

It's when I don't look that it happens.

MARIA

I think I will tell Mama and Papa about you and 'Nardo in the balcony of the movies.

ANITA

I'll rip this to shreds!

MARIA

No. But if you perhaps could manage to lower the neck—

ANITA

Next year.

MARIA

Next year I will be married and no one will care if it is down to here!

ANITA

Down to where?

MARIA

Down to here. (*Indicates her waist*) I hate this dress!

ANITA

Then don't wear it and don't come with us to the dance.

MARIA

(*Shocked*)

Don't come! (*Grabs the dress*) Could we not dye it red, at least?

ANITA

No, we could not.

(*She starts to help* MARIA *into the dress.*)

MARIA

White is for babies. I will be the only one there in a white—

ANITA

Well???

MARIA

Ahhhh—*sí!* It is a beautiful dress: I love you!

(*As she hugs* ANITA, BERNARDO *enters, followed by a shy, gentle sweet-faced boy:* CHINO.)

BERNARDO

Are you ready?

MARIA

Come in, 'Nardo. (*Whirls in the dress*) Is it not beautiful?

BERNARDO

(*Looking only at* MARIA'S *face*)

Yes. (*Kisses her*) Very.

ANITA

I didn't quite hear . . .

BERNARDO

(*Kissing* ANITA *quite differently*)

Very beautiful.

MARIA

(*Watches them a second, then turns to* CHINO)

Come in, Chino. Do not be afraid.

CHINO

But this is a shop for ladies.

BERNARDO

Our ladies!

MARIA

'Nardo, it is most important that I have a wonderful time at the dancing tonight.

BERNARDO

(*As* ANITA *hooks up* MARIA)

Why?

MARIA

Because tonight is the real beginning of my life as a young lady of America!

(*She begins to whirl in the dress as the shop slides off and a flood of gaily colored streamers pours down. As* MARIA *begins to turn and turn, going offstage, Shark girls, dressed for the dance whirl on, followed by Jet girls, by boys from both gangs. The streamers fly up again for the next scene.*)

Scene 4

10:00 P.M. *The gym.*

Actually, a converted gymnasium of a settlement house, at the moment being used as a dancehall, disguised for the occasion with streamers and bunting.

Both gangs are jitterbugging wildly with their bodies, but their faces, although they are enjoying themselves, remain cool, almost detached. The line between the two gangs is sharply defined by the colors they wear: the Jets, girls as well as boys, reflecting the colors of the Jet jackets; the same is true of the Sharks. The dancing is a physical and emotional release for these kids.

MARIA *enters with* CHINO, BERNARDO *and* ANITA. *As she looks around, delighted, thrilled by this, her first dance, the Jets catch sight of* BERNARDO, *who is being greeted by* PEPE, *his lieutenant, and other Sharks. As the music peters away, the Jets withdraw to one side of the hall, around* RIFF. *The Sharks seeing this, draw to their side, around* BERNARDO. *A brief consultation, and* RIFF *starts across—with lieutenants—to make his challenge to* BERNARDO, *who starts—with his lieutenants—to meet him. The moment is brief but it would be disastrous if a smiling, overly cheerful young man of about thirty did not hurry forward. He is called* GLAD HAND, *and he is a "square."*

GLAD HAND

(*Beaming*)

All right, boys and girls! Attention, please! (*Hum of talk*) Attention! (KRUPKE *appears behind* GLAD HAND: *the talk stops*) Thank you. It sure is a fine turnout tonight. (*Ad libs from the kids*) We want you to make friends here, so we're going to have a few get-together dances. (*Ad libs: "Oh, ginger peachy," etc.*) You form two circles: boys on the outside, girls on the inside.

SNOWBOY

Where are you?

GLAD HAND

(*Tries to laugh at this*)

All right. Now when the music stops, each boy dances with whichever girl is opposite. O.K.? O.K. Two circles, kids. (*The* KIDS *clap their hands back at him and ad lib: "Two circles, kids," etc., but do not move*) Well, it won't hurt you to try.

SNOWBOY

(*Limping forward*)

Oh, it hurts; it hurts; it—

(KRUPKE *steps forward.* SNOWBOY *straightens up and meekly returns to his place.* RIFF *steps forward and beckons to his girl,* VELMA. *She is terribly young, sexy, lost in a world of jive. She slithers forward to take her place with* RIFF. *The challenge is met by* BERNARDO, *who steps forward, leading* ANITA *as though he were presenting the most magnificent lady in all the world. The other kids follow, forming the two circles* GLAD HAND *requested.*)

GLAD HAND

That's it, kids. Keep the ball rolling. Round she goes and where she stops, nobody knows. All right: here we go!

(*Promenade music starts and the circles start revolving.* GLAD HAND, *whistle to his mouth, is in the center with* KRUPKE. *He blows the whistle and the music stops, leaving Jet boys opposite Shark girls, and vice versa. There is a moment of tenseness, then* BERNARDO *reaches across the Jet girl opposite for* ANITA's *hand, and she comes to him.* RIFF *reaches for* VELMA; *and the kids of both gangs follow suit. The "get-together" has failed, and each gang is on its own side of the hall as a mambo starts. This turns into a challenge dance between* BERNARDO *and* ANITA*—cheered on by the Sharks—and* RIFF *and* VELMA*—cheered on by the Jets. During it,* TONY *enters and is momentarily embraced by* RIFF, *who is delighted that his best friend did turn up. The dance builds wilder and wilder, until, at the peak, everybody is dancing and shouting, "Go, Mambo!" It is at this moment that* TONY *and* MARIA*—at opposite sides of the hall—see each other. They have been cheering on their respective friends, clapping in rhythm. Now, as they see each other, their voices die, their smiles fade, their hands slowly go to their sides. The lights fade on the others, who disappear into the haze of the background as a delicate cha-cha begins and* TONY *and* MARIA *slowly walk forward to meet each other. Slowly, as though in a dream, they drift into the steps of the dance, always looking at each other, completely lost in each other; unaware of anyone, any place, any time, anything but one another.*)

TONY

You're not thinking I'm someone else?

MARIA

I know you are not.

TONY

Or that we have met before?

MARIA

I know we have not.

TONY

I felt, I *knew* something-never-before was going to happen, had to happen. But this is—

MARIA

(*Interrupting*)

My hands are cold. (*He takes them in his*) Yours, too. (*He moves her hands to his face*) So warm.

(*She moves his hands to her face.*)

TONY

Yours, too.

MARIA

But of course. They are the same.

TONY

It's so much to believe—you're not joking me?

MARIA

I have not yet learned how to joke that way. I think now I never will.

(*Impulsively, he stops to kiss her hands; then tenderly, innocently, her lips. The music bursts out, the lights flare up, and* BERNARDO *is upon them in an icy rage.*)

BERNARDO

Go home, "*American*."

TONY

Slow down, Bernardo.

BERNARDO

Stay away from my sister!

TONY

. . . Sister?

(RIFF *steps up.*)

BERNARDO

(*To* MARIA)

Couldn't you see he's one of them?

MARIA

No; I saw only him.

BERNARDO

(*As* CHINO *comes up*)

I told you: there's only one thing they want from a Puerto Rican girl!

TONY

That's a lie!

RIFF

Cool, boy.

CHINO

(*To* TONY)

Get away.

TONY

You keep out, Chino. (*To* MARIA) Don't listen to them!

BERNARDO

She will listen to her brother before—

RIFF

(*Overlapping*)

If you characters want to settle—

GLAD HAND

Please! Everything was going so well! Do you fellows get pleasure out of making trouble? Now come on—it won't hurt you to have a good time.

(*Music starts again.* BERNARDO *is on one side with* MARIA *and* CHINO; ANITA *joins them.* TONY *is on the other with* RIFF *and* DIESEL. *Light emphasizes the first group.*)

BERNARDO

I warned you—

CHINO

Do not yell at her, 'Nardo.

BERNARDO

You yell at babies.

ANITA

And put ideas in the baby's head.

BERNARDO

Take her home, Chino.

MARIA

'Nardo, it is my first dance.

BERNARDO

Please. We are family, Maria. Go.

(MARIA *hesitates, then starts out with* CHINO *as the light follows her to the other group, which she passes.*)

RIFF

(*To* DIESEL, *indicating* TONY *happily*)

I guess the kid's with us for sure now.

(TONY *doesn't even hear; he is staring at* MARIA, *who stops for a moment.*)

CHINO

Come, Maria.

(*They continue out.*)

TONY

Maria . . .

(*He is unaware that* BERNARDO *is crossing toward him, but* RIFF *intercepts.*)

BERNARDO

I don't want you.

RIFF

I want you, though. For a war council—Jets and Sharks.

BERNARDO

The pleasure is mine.

RIFF

Let's go outside.

BERNARDO

I would not leave the ladies here alone. We will meet you in half an hour.

RIFF

Doc's drugstore? (BERNARDO *nods*) And no jazz before then.

BERNARDO

I understand the rules—Native Boy.

(*The light is fading on them, on everyone but* TONY.)

RIFF

Spread the word, Diesel.

DIESEL

Right, Daddy-o.

RIFF

Let's get the chicks and kick it. Tony?

TONY

Maria . . .

(*Music starts.*)

RIFF

(*In darkness*)

Tony!

DIESEL

(*In darkness*)

Ah, we'll see him at Doc's.

TONY

(*Speaking dreamily over the music—he is now standing alone in the light*)

Maria . . .

(*Singing softly*)

The most beautiful sound I ever heard.

(VOICES *offstage*)

Maria, Maria, Maria, Maria . . .

(TONY)

All the beautiful sounds of the world in a single word:

(VOICES *offstage*)

Maria, Maria, Maria, Maria . . .

(*Swelling in intensity*)

Maria, Maria . . .

(TONY)

Maria!
I've just met a girl named Maria,
And suddenly that name
Will never be the same
To me.

Maria!
I've just kissed a girl named Maria,
And suddenly I've found
How wonderful a sound
Can be!

Maria!
Say it loud and there's music playing—
Say it soft and it's almost like praying—
Maria . . .
I'll never stop saying
Maria!

(CHORUS, *offstage, against* TONY's *obbligato*)

I've just met a girl named Maria,
And suddenly that name
Will never be the same
To me.
Maria—
I've just kissed a girl named Maria,
And suddenly I've found
How wonderful a sound
Can be!

(TONY)

Maria—
Say it loud and there's music playing—
Say it soft and it's almost like praying—

Maria—
I'll never stop saying Maria!
The most beautiful sound I ever heard—
Maria.

(*During the song, the stage behind* TONY *has gone dark; by the time he has finished, it is set for the next scene.*)

SCENE 5

11:00 P.M. *A back alley.*

A suggestion of buildings; a fire escape climbing to the rear window of an unseen flat.

As TONY *sings, he looks for where* MARIA *lives, wishing for her. And she does appear, at the window above him, which opens onto the fire escape. Music stays beneath most of the scene.*

(TONY *sings*)

Maria, Maria . . .

MARIA

Ssh!

TONY

Maria!!

MARIA

Quiet!

TONY

Come down.

MARIA

No.

TONY

Maria . . .

MARIA

Please. If Bernardo—

TONY

He's at the dance. Come down.

MARIA

He will soon bring Anita home.

TONY

Just for a minute.

MARIA

(*Smiles*)

A minute is not enough.

TONY

(*Smiles*)

For an hour, then.

MARIA

I cannot.

TONY

Forever!

MARIA

Ssh!

TONY

Then I'm coming up.

WOMAN'S VOICE

(*From the offstage apartment*)

Maria!

MARIA

Momentito, Mama . . .

TONY

(*Climbing up*)

Maria, Maria—

MARIA

Cállate! (*Reaching her hand out to stop him*) Ssh!

TONY

(*Grabbing her hand*)

Ssh!

MARIA

It is dangerous.

TONY

I'm *not* "one of them."

MARIA

You are; but to me, you are not. Just as I am one of them—
(*She gestures toward the apartment.*)

TONY

To me, you are all the—
(*She covers his mouth with her hand.*)

MAN'S VOICE

(*From the unseen apartment*)

Maruca!

MARIA

Sí, ya vengo, Papa.

TONY

Maruca?

MARIA

His pet name for me.

TONY

I like him. He will like me.

MARIA

No. He is like Bernardo: afraid. (*Suddenly laughing*) Imagine being afraid of you!

TONY

You see?

MARIA

(*Touching his face*)

I see you.

TONY

See only me.

(MARIA *sings*)

Only you, you're the only thing I'll see forever.
In my eyes, in my words and in everything I do,
Nothing else but you
Ever!

(TONY)

And there's nothing for me but Maria,
Every sight that I see is Maria.

(MARIA)

Tony, Tony . . .

(TONY)

Always you, every thought I'll ever know,
Everywhere I go, you'll be.

(MARIA)

All the world is only you and me!

(*And now the buildings, the world fade away, leaving them suspended in space*)

Tonight, tonight,
It all began tonight,
I saw you and the world went away.
Tonight, tonight,
There's only you tonight,
What you are, what you do, what you say.

(TONY)

Today, all day I had the feeling
A miracle would happen—
I know now I was right.
For here you are
And what was just a world is a star
Tonight!

(BOTH)

Tonight, tonight,
The world is full of light,
With suns and moons all over the place.
Tonight, tonight,
The world is wild and bright,
Going mad, shooting sparks into space.
Today the world was just an address,
A place for me to live in,
No better than all right,

But here you are
And what was just a world is a star
Tonight!

MAN'S VOICE

(Offstage)

Maruca!

MARIA

Wait for me!

(She goes inside as the buildings begin to come back into place.)

(TONY *sings*)

Tonight, tonight,
It all began tonight,
I saw you and the world went away.

MARIA

(Returning)

I cannot stay. Go quickly!

TONY

I'm not afraid.

MARIA

They are strict with me. Please.

TONY

(Kissing her)

Good night.

MARIA

Buenas noches.

TONY

I love you.

MARIA

Yes, yes. Hurry. (*He climbs down*) Wait! When will I see you? (*He starts back up*) No!

TONY

Tomorrow.

MARIA

I work at the bridal shop. Come there.

TONY

At sundown.

MARIA

Yes. Good night.

TONY

Good night.

(*He starts off.*)

MARIA

Tony!

TONY

Ssh!

MARIA

Come to the back door.

TONY

Sí.

(*Again, he starts out.*)

MARIA

Tony! (*He stops. A pause*) What does Tony stand for?

TONY

Anton.

MARIA

Te adoro, Anton.

TONY

Te adoro, Maria.

(BOTH *sing as music starts again*)

Good night, good night,
Sleep well and when you dream,
Dream of me
Tonight.

(*She goes inside; He ducks out into the shadows just as* BERNARDO *and* ANITA *enter, followed by* INDIO, *and* PEPE *and their girls. One is a bleached-blond, bangled beauty:* CONSUELO. *The other, more quietly dressed, is* ROSALIA. *She is not too bright.*)

BERNARDO

(*Looking up to the window*)

Maria?

ANITA

She *has* a mother. Also a father.

BERNARDO

They do not know this country any better than she does.

ANITA

You do not know it at all! Girls here are free to have fun. She-is-in-America-now.

BERNARDO

(Exaggerated)

But Puerto-Rico-is-in-America-now!

ANITA

(In disgust)

Ai!

BERNARDO

(Cooing)

Anita Josefina Teresita—

ANITA

It's plain Anita now—

BERNARDO

(Continuing through)

—Beatriz del Carmen Margarita, etcetera, etcetera—

ANITA

Immigrant!

BERNARDO

(Pulling her to him)

Thank God, you can't change your hair!

PEPE

(Fondling CONSUELO's *bleached mop)*

Is that possible?

CONSUELO

In the U.S.A., everything is real.

BERNARDO

(*To* CHINO, *who enters*)

Chino, how was she when you took her home?

CHINO

All right. 'Nardo, she was only dancing.

BERNARDO

With an "*American*." Who is really a Polack.

ANITA

Says the Spic.

BERNARDO

You are not so cute.

ANITA

That Tony is.

ROSALIA

And he works.

CHINO

A delivery boy.

ANITA

And what are you?

CHINO

An assistant.

BERNARDO

Sí! And Chino makes half what the Polack makes—the Polack is American!

ANITA

Ai! Here comes the whole commercial! (*A burlesque oration in mock Puerto Rican accent.* BERNARDO *starts the first line with her*) The mother of Tony was born in Poland; the father still goes to night school. Tony was born in America, so that makes him an American. But us? Foreigners!

PEPE *and* CONSUELO

Lice!

PEPE, CONSUELO, ANITA

Cockroaches!

BERNARDO

Well, it is true! You remember how we were when we first came! Did we even think of going back?

BERNARDO *and* ANITA

No! We came ready, eager—

ANITA

(*Mocking*)

With our hearts open—

CONSUELO

Our arms open—

PEPE

You came with your pants open.

CONSUELO

You did, pig! (*Slaps him*) You'll go back with handcuffs!

BERNARDO

I am going back with a Cadillac!

CHINO

Air-conditioned!

BERNARDO

Built-in bar!

CHINO

Telephone!

BERNARDO

Television!

CHINO

Compatible color!

BERNARDO

And a king-sized bed. (*Grabs* ANITA) Come on.

ANITA

(*Mimicking*)

Come on.

BERNARDO

Well, are you or aren't you?

ANITA

Well, are you or aren't you?

BERNARDO

Well, are you?

ANITA

You have your big, important war council. The council or me?

BERNARDO

First one, then the other.

ANITA

(*Breaking away from him*)

I am an American girl now. I don't wait.

BERNARDO

(*To* CHINO)

Back home, women know their place.

ANITA

Back home, little boys don't have war councils.

BERNARDO

You want me to be an American? (*To the boys*) *Vámonos, chicos, Es tarde.* (*A mock bow*) *Buenos noches,* Anita Josefina del Carmen, etcetera, etcetera, etcetera.

(*He exits with the boys.*)

ROSALIA

That's a very pretty name: Etcetera.

ANITA

Ai!

CONSUELO

She means well.

ROSALIA

We have many pretty names at home.

ANITA

(Mimicking)

At home, at home. If it's so nice "at home," why don't you go back there?

ROSALIA

I would like to—*(A look from* ANITA*)*—just for a successful visit.

(She sings nostalgically)

Puerto Rico . . .
You lovely island . . .
Island of tropical breezes.
Always the pineapples growing,
Always the coffee blossoms blowing . . .

(ANITA *sings sarcastically)*

Puerto Rico . . .
You ugly island . . .
Island of tropic diseases.
Always the hurricanes blowing,
Always the population growing . . .
And the money owing,
And the babies crying,
And the bullets flying.
I like the island Manhattan—
Smoke on your pipe and put that in!

(ALL, *except* ROSALIA)

I like to be in America!
O.K. by me in America!
Everything free in America
For a small fee in America!

(ROSALIA)

I like the city of San Juan—

(ANITA)

I know a boat you can get on.

(ROSALIA)

Hundreds of flowers in full bloom—

(ANITA)

Hundreds of people in each room!

(ALL, *except* ROSALIA)

Automobile in America,
Chromium steel in America,
Wire-spoke wheel in America—
Very big deal in America!

(ROSALIA)

I'll drive a Buick through San Juan—

(ANITA)

If there's a road you can drive on.

(ROSALIA)

I'll give my cousins a free ride—

(ANITA)

How you get all of them inside?

(ALL, *except* ROSALIA)
Immigrant goes to America,
Many hellos in America;
Nobody knows in America
Puerto Rico's in America.
(*The girls whistle and dance.*)

(ROSALIA)
When I will go back to San Juan—

(ANITA)
When you will shut up and get gone!

(ROSALIA)
I'll give them new washing machine—

(ANITA)
What have they got there to keep clean?

(ALL, *except* ROSALIA)
I like the shores of America!
Comfort is yours in America!
Knobs on the doors in America,
Wall-to-wall floors in America!
(*They whistle and dance.*)

(ROSALIA)
I'll bring a TV to San Juan—

(ANITA)
If there's a current to turn on.

(ROSALIA)
Everyone there will give big cheer!

(ANITA)

Everyone there will have moved here!

(*The song ends in a joyous dance.*)

The Lights Black Out

Scene 6

Midnight. The drugstore.

A suggestion of a run-down, musty general store which, in cities, is called a drugstore. A door leading to the street outside; another leading to the cellar below.

BABY JOHN *is reading a comic book;* A-RAB *is playing solitaire;* ANYBODYS *is huddled by the juke box;* ACTION *is watching the street door. The atmosphere is tense, jumpy.* ACTION *slams the door and strides to the dart board.*

ACTION

Where the devil are they? Are we havin' a war council tonight or ain't we?

(*He throws a dart savagely.*)

BABY JOHN

He don't use knives. He don't even use an atomic ray gun.

A-RAB

Who don't?

BABY JOHN

Superman. Gee, I love him.

SNOWBOY

So marry him.

ANYBODYS

I ain't never gonna get married: too noisy.

A-RAB

You ain't never gonna get married: too ugly.

ANYBODYS

(*"Shooting" him*)

Pow pow!

A-RAB

Cracko, jacko! (*Clutching his belly, he spins to the floor*) Down goes a teen-age hoodlum.

BABY JOHN

Could a zip gun make you do like that?

(*A second of silence. Then* SNOWBOY *slams into the room and they all jump.*)

ACTION

What the hell's a matter with you?

SNOWBOY

I got caught sneakin' outa the movies.

A-RAB

Sneakin' *out?* Wadd'ya do that for?

SNOWBOY

I sneaked in.

ACTION

A war council comin' up and he goes to the movies.

ANYBODYS

And you let him be a Jet!

BABY JOHN

Ah, go walk the streets like ya sister.

ANYBODYS

(*Jumping him*)

Lissen, jail bait, I licked you twice and I can do it again.

(*From the doorway behind the counter a little middle-aged man enters:* DOC.)

DOC

Curfew, gentlemen. And lady. Baby John, you should be home in bed.

BABY JOHN

We're gonna have a war council here, Doc.

DOC

A who?

A-RAB

To decide on weapons for a big-time rumble!

SNOWBOY

We're gonna mix with the PRs.

DOC

Weapons. You couldn't play basketball?

ANYBODYS

Get with it, buddy boy.

DOC

War councils—

ACTION

Don't start, Doc.

DOC

Rumbles . . .

ACTION

Doc—

DOC

Why, when I was your age—

ACTION

When you was my age; when my old man was my age; when my brother was my age! *You was never my age, none a you!* The sooner you creeps get hip to that, the sooner you'll dig us.

DOC

I'll dig your early graves, that's what I'll dig.

A-RAB

Dig, dig, dig—

DOC

What're you gonna be when you grow up?

ANYBODYS

(*Wistfully*)

A telephone call girl!

(*The store doorbell tinkles as* RIFF *enters with* VELMA.)

SNOWBOY

Riff, hey!

ACTION

Are they comin'?

RIFF

Unwind, Action. Hey, Doc, Tony here?

DOC

No, Riff, it's closing time.

ACTION

(*To* RIFF)

What d'ya think they're gonna ask for?

A-RAB

Just rubbers hoses, maybe, huh?

RIFF

Cool, little men. Easy, freezy cool.

VELMA

Oo, oo, ooblee—oo.

(DIESEL *enters with a would-be grand number:* GRAZIELLA.)

DIESEL

They're comin' any minute now!

ACTION

Chung chung!

A-RAB

Cracko, jacko!

VELMA

Ooblee-oo.

RIFF

(*Sharply*)

Cool!

ANYBODYS

Riff—in a tight spot you need every man you can—

RIFF

No.

GRAZIELLA

(*Indicating* ANYBODYS *to* VELMA)

An American tragedy.

ANYBODYS

(*"Shooting" her*)

Pow.

GRAZIELLA

Poo.

VELMA

Ooblee-pooh.

(*They giggle.*)

RIFF

Now when the victims come in, you chicks cut out.

GRAZIELLA

We might, and then again we might not.

DIESEL

This ain't kid stuff, Graziella.

GRAZIELLA

I and Velma ain't kid stuff, neither. Are we, Vel?

VELMA

No thank you-oo, ooblee-oo.

GRAZIELLA

And you can punctuate it?

VELMA

Ooo!

(*They giggle again.*)

ACTION

(*To* RIFF)

What're we poopin' around with dumb broads?

GRAZIELLA

(*Enraged*)

I and Velma ain't dumb!

ACTION

We got important business comin'.

DOC

Makin' trouble for the Puerto Ricans?

SNOWBOY

They make trouble for us.

DOC

Look! He almost laughs when he says it. For you, trouble is a relief.

RIFF

We've got to stand up to the PRs, Doc. It's important.

DOC

Fighting over a little piece of the street is so important?

ACTION

To us, it is.

DOC

To hoodlums, it is.

(*He goes out through the cellar doorway as* ACTION *lunges for him.*)

ACTION

Don't you call me hoodlum!

RIFF

(*Holding him*)

Easy, Action! Save your steam for the rumble.

A-RAB

He don't want what we want, so we're hoodlums!

BABY JOHN

I wear a jacket like my buddies, so my teacher calls me hoodlum!

ACTION

I swear the next creep who calls me hoodlum—

RIFF

You'll laugh! Yeah. Now you all better dig this and dig it the most. No matter who or what is eatin' at you, you show it, buddy boys, and *you are dead*. You are cuttin' a hole in yourselves for them to stick in a red hot umbrella and open it. Wide. You wanna live? You play it cool.

(*Music starts.*)

ACTION

I wanna get even!

RIFF

Get cool.

A-RAB

I wanna bust!

RIFF

Bust cool.

BABY JOHN

I wanna go!

RIFF

Go cool!

(*He sings*)

Boy, boy, crazy boy—
Get cool, boy!
Got a rocket in your pocket—
Keep coolly cool, boy!
Don't get hot,
'Cause, man, you got
Some high times ahead.
Take it slow and, Daddy-o,
You can live it up and die in bed!

Boy, boy, crazy boy—
    Stay loose, boy!
Breeze it, buzz it, easy does it—
    Turn off the juice, boy!
        Go man, go,
        But not like a yo-
        Yo school boy—
        Just play it cool, boy,
Real cool!

Easy, Action.
Easy.

(This leads into a frenetic dance in which the boys and girls release their emotions and get "cool." It finishes, starts again when a Jet bounces in with the gang whistle. Everyone but RIFF *and* VELMA *stops dancing. A moment, then* BERNARDO, CHINO, PEPE *and* INDIO *enter. The tinkle of the doorbell brings a worried* DOC *back in. Tension—but* RIFF *dances a moment longer. Then he pats* VELMA *on her behind. Followed by* GRAZIELLA, *she runs out, slithering past the Sharks.* ANYBODYS *is back, huddled by the juke box, but* RIFF *spots her. She gives him a pleading let-me-stay look, but he gestures for her to go. Unlike the other girls, as she exits,* ANYBODYS *shoves the Sharks like a big tough man.)*

RIFF

Set 'em up, Doc. Cokes all around.

BERNARDO

Let's get down to business.

RIFF

Bernardo hasn't learned the procedures of gracious livin'.

BERNARDO

I don't like you, either. So cut it.

RIFF

Kick it, Doc.

DOC

Boys, couldn't you maybe all talk it—

RIFF

Kick it!

(DOC *goes out. The two gangs take places behind their leaders.*)

RIFF

We challenge you to a rumble. All out, once and for all. Accept?

BERNARDO

On what terms?

RIFF

Whatever terms you're callin', buddy boy. You crossed the line once too often.

BERNARDO

You started it.

RIFF

Who jumped A-rab this afternoon?

BERNARDO

Who jumped me the first day I moved here?

ACTION

Who asked you to move here?

PEPE

Who asked you?

SNOWBOY

Move where you're wanted!

A-RAB

Back where ya came from!

ACTION

Spics!

PEPE

Micks!

INDIO

Wop!

BERNARDO

We accept!

RIFF

Time:

BERNARDO

Tomorrow?

RIFF

After dark. (*They shake*) Place:

BERNARDO

The park.

RIFF

The river.

BERNARDO

Under the highway.

(*They shake.*)

RIFF

Weapons:

(*The doorbell tinkles as* TONY *bursts in, yelling.*)

TONY

Hey, Doc!

(*He stops as he sees them. Silence. Then he comes forward.*)

RIFF

Weapons!

(DOC *enters.*)

BERNARDO

Weapons . . .

RIFF

You call.

BERNARDO

Your challenge.

RIFF

Afraid to call?

BERNARDO

. . . . Sticks.

RIFF

. . . . Rocks.

BERNARDO

. . . Poles.

RIFF

. . . Cans.

BERNARDO

. . Bricks.

RIFF

. . Bats.

BERNARDO

. Clubs.

RIFF

Chains.

TONY

Bottles, knives, guns! (*They stare*) What a coop full of chickens!

ACTION

Who you callin' chicken?

BERNARDO

Every dog knows his own.

TONY

I'm callin' all of you chicken. The big tough buddy boys have to throw bricks! Afraid to get close in? Afraid to slug it out? Afraid to use plain skin?

BABY JOHN

Not even garbage?

ACTION

That ain't a rumble.

RIFF

Who says?

BERNARDO

You said call weapons.

TONY

A rumble can be clinched by a fair fight. If you have the guts to risk that. Best man from each gang to slug it out.

BERNARDO

(*Looking at* TONY)

I'd enjoy to risk that. O.K.! Fair fight!

PEPE

What?

ACTION

(*Simultaneously*)

No!

RIFF

The commanders say yes or no. (*To* BERNARDO) Fair fight.
(*They shake.*)

BERNARDO

(*To* TONY)

In two minutes you will be like a fish after skinnin'.

RIFF

Your best man fights our best man—and we pick him.

(*Claps* DIESEL *on the shoulder.*)

BERNARDO

But I thought I would be—

RIFF

We shook on it, Bernardo.

BERNARDO

Yes. I shook on it.

ACTION

(*Quickly*)

Look, Bernardo, if you wanna change your mind, maybe we could all—

(*One of the Jets near the door suddenly whistles. Instantly, they shift positions so they are mixed up: no segregation. Silence; then in comes* SCHRANK. *During the following, the gangs are absolutely silent and motionless, unless otherwise indicated.*)

DOC

(*Unhappily*)

Good evening, Lieutenant Schrank. I and Tony was just closing up.

SCHRANK

(*Lifting a pack of cigarettes*)

Mind?

DOC

I have no mind. I am the village idiot.

SCHRANK

(Lighting a cigarette)

I always make it a rule to smoke in the can. And what else is a room with half-breeds in it, eh, Riff? (BERNARDO's *move is checked by* RIFF. SCHRANK *speaks again, pleasantly*) Clear out, Spics. Sure; it's a free country and I ain't got the right. But it's a country with laws: and I can find the right. I got the badge, you got the skin. It's tough all over. Beat it! (*A second. Then* RIFF *nods once to* BERNARDO, *who nods to his gang. Slowly, they file out.* BERNARDO *starts to whistle "My Country 'Tis of Thee" as he exits proudly. His gang joins in, finishing a sardonic jazz lick offstage.* SCHRANK, *still pleasant*) From their angle, sure. Say, where's the rumble gonna be? Ah, look: I know regular Americans don't rub with the gold-teeth otherwise. The river? The park? (*Silence*) I'm for *you*. I want this beat cleaned up and you can do it for me. I'll even lend a hand if it gets rough. Where ya gonna rumble? The playground? Sweeney's lot? (*Angered by the silence*) Ya think I'm a lousy stool pigeon? I wanna help ya get rid of them! Come on! Where's it gonna be? . . . Get smart, you stupid hoodlums! I oughta fine ya for litterin' the streets. You oughta be taken down the station house and have your skulls mashed to a pulp! You and the tin-horn immigrant scum you come from! How's your old man's d.t.'s, A-rab? How's the action on your mother's mattress, Action? (ACTION *lunges for him but is tripped up by* RIFF. SCHRANK *crouches low, ready for him. Quiet now*) Let him go, buddy boy, just let him go. (ACTION *starts to his feet but* DIESEL *holds him*) One of these days there won't be nobody to hold you. (RIFF *deliberately starts for the door, followed by the others, except* TONY) I'll find out where ya gonna rumble. But be sure to finish each other off. Because if you don't, I will! (RIFF *has stayed at the door until the others have passed through. Now he just looks at* SCHRANK *and cockily saunters out. Silence.* SCHRANK *looks at* DOC) Well, you try keepin' hoodlums in line and see what it does to you.

(*He exits.*)

DOC

(*Indicating* SCHRANK)

It wouldn't give me a mouth like his.

TONY

Forget him. From here on in, everything goes my way.

(*He starts to clean up, to turn out the lights.*)

DOC

You think it'll really be a fair fight.

TONY

Yeah.

DOC

What have you been takin' tonight?

TONY

A trip to the moon. And I'll tell you a secret. It isn't a man that's up there, Doc. It's a girl, a lady. (*Opens the door*) *Buenas noches, señor.*

DOC

Buenas noches?! So that's why you made it a fair fight. (TONY *smiles*) . . . Tony . . . things aren't tough enough?

TONY

Tough? Doc, I'm in love.

DOC

How do you know?

TONY

Because . . . there isn't any other way I could feel.

DOC

And you're not frightened?

TONY

Should I be?

(*He opens door, exits.*)

DOC

Why? I'm frightened enough for both of you.

(*He turns out the last light.*)

The Stage Is Dark

SCENE 7

5:30 P.M. *The next day. The bridal shop*

Hot late-afternoon sun coloring the workroom. One or two sewing machines. Several dressmaker dummies, male and female, in bridal-party garb.

MARIA, *in a smock, is hand-sewing a wedding veil as* ANITA *whirls in whipping off her smock.*

ANITA

She's gone! That old bag of a *bruja* has gone!

MARIA

Bravo!

ANITA

The day is over, the jail is open, home we go!

MARIA

You go, *querida*. I will lock up.

ANITA

Finish tomorrow. Come!

MARIA

But I am in no hurry.

ANITA

I am. I'm going to take a bubble bath all during supper: Black Orchid.

MARIA

You will not eat?

ANITA

After the rumble—with 'Nardo.

MARIA

(*Sewing, angrily*)

That rumble, why do they have it?

ANITA

You saw how they dance: like they have to get rid of something, quick. That's how they fight.

MARIA

To get rid of what?

ANITA

Too much feeling. And they get rid of it: after a fight, that brother of yours is so healthy! Definitely: Black Orchid.

(*There is a knock at rear door, and* TONY *enters.*)

TONY

Buenas noches!

ANITA

(*Sarcastically, to* MARIA)

"You go, *querida*. I will lock up." (*To* TONY) It's too early for *noches. Buenas tardes.*

TONY

(*Bows*)

Gracias. Buenas tardes.

MARIA

He just came to deliver aspirin.

ANITA

You'll need it.

TONY

No, we're out of the world.

ANITA

You're out of your heads.

TONY

We're twelve feet in the air.

MARIA

(*Gently taking his hand*)

Anita can see all that. (*To* ANITA) You will not tell?

ANITA

Tell what? How can I hear what goes on twelve feet over my head? (*Opens door. To* MARIA) You better be home in fifteen minutes.

(*She goes out.*)

TONY

Don't worry. She likes us!

MARIA

But she is worried.

TONY

She's foolish. We're untouchable; we *are* in the air; we have magic!

MARIA

Magic is also evil and black. Are you going to that rumble?

TONY

No.

MARIA

Yes.

TONY

Why??

MARIA

You must go and stop it.

TONY

I have stopped it! It's only a fist fight. 'Nardo won't get—

MARIA

Any fight is not good for us.

TONY

Everything is good for us and we are good for everything.

MARIA

Listen and *hear* me. You must go and stop it.

TONY

Then I will.

MARIA

(*Surprised*)

Can you?

TONY

You don't want even a fist fight? There won't be any fight.

MARIA

I believe you! You *do* have magic.

TONY

Of course, I have you. You go home and dress up. Then tonight, I will come by for you.

MARIA

You cannot come by. My mama . . .

TONY

(*After a pause*)

Then I will take you to my house—

MARIA

(*Shaking her head*)

Your mama . . .

(*Another awkward pause. Then he sees a female dummy and pushes it forward.*)

TONY

She will come running from the kitchen to welcome you. She lives in the kitchen.

MARIA

Dressed so elegant?

TONY

I told her you were coming. She will look at your face and try not to smile. And she will say: Skinny—but pretty.

MARIA

She is plump, no doubt.

TONY

(*Holding out the waist of dummy's dress*)

Fat!

MARIA

(*Indicating another female dummy*)

I take after my mama; delicate-boned. (*He kisses her*) Not in front of Mama! (*He turns the dummy around as she goes to a male dummy*) Oh, I would like to see Papa in this! Mama will make him ask about your prospects, if you go to church. But Papa—Papa *might* like you.

TONY

(*Kneeling to the "father" dummy*)

May I have your daughter's hand?

MARIA

He says yes.

TONY

Gracias!

MARIA

And your mama?

TONY

I'm afraid to ask her.

MARIA

Tell her she's not getting a daughter; she's getting rid of a son!

TONY

She says yes.

MARIA

She has good taste.

(*She grabs up the wedding veil and puts it on as* TONY *arranges the dummies.*)

TONY

Maid of honor!

MARIA

That color is bad for Anita.

TONY

Best man!

MARIA

That is my Papa!

TONY

Sorry, Papa. Here we go, Riff: Womb to Tomb!

(*He takes hat off dummy.*)

MARIA

Now you see, Anita, I told you there was nothing to worry about.

(*Music starts as she leaves the dummy and walks up to* TONY. *They look at each other—and the play acting vanishes. Slowly, seriously, they turn front, and together kneel as before an altar.*)

TONY

I, Anton, take thee, Maria . . .

BRIDAL

MARIA

I, Maria, take thee, Anton . . .

TONY

For richer, for poorer . . .

MARIA

In sickness and in health . . .

TONY

To love and to honor . . .

MARIA

To hold and to keep . . .

TONY

From each sun to each moon . . .

MARIA

From tomorrow to tomorrow . . .

TONY

From now to forever . . .

MARIA

Till death do us part.

TONY

With this ring, I thee wed.

MARIA

With this ring, I thee wed.

(TONY *sings*)

Make of our hands one hand,
Make of our hearts one heart,
Make of our vows one last vow:
Only death will part us now.

(MARIA)

Make of our lives one life,
Day after day, one life.

(BOTH)

Now it begins, now we start
One hand, one heart—
Even death won't part us now.

(They look at each other, then at the reality of their "game." They smile tenderly, ruefully, and slowly put the dummies back into position. Though brought back to earth, they continue to sing.)

Make of our lives one life,
Day after day, one life.
Now it begins, now we start
One hand, one heart—
Even death won't part us now.

(Very gently, he kisses her hand.)

The Lights Fade Out.

SCENE 8

6:00 to 9:00 P.M. *The neighborhood.*

Spotlights pick out RIFF *and the Jets,* BERNARDO *and the Sharks,* ANITA, MARIA *and* TONY *against small sets representing different places in the neighborhood. All are waiting expectantly for the coming of night, but for very different reasons.*

(JETS *sing*)

The Jets are gonna have their day
Tonight.

(SHARKS)

The Sharks are gonna have their way
Tonight.

(JETS)

The Puerto Ricans grumble,
"Fair fight."
But if they start a rumble,
We'll rumble 'em right.

(SHARKS)

We're gonna hand 'em a surprise
Tonight.

(JETS)

We're gonna cut 'em down to size
Tonight.

(SHARKS)

We said, "O.K., no rumpus,
No tricks"—
But just in case they jump us,
We're ready to mix
Tonight!

(BOTH GANGS)

We're gonna rock it tonight,
We're gonna jazz it up and have us a ball.
They're gonna get it tonight;
The more they turn it on, the harder they'll fall!

(JETS)

Well, they began it—

(SHARKS)

Well, they began it—

(BOTH GANGS)

And we're the ones to stop 'em once and for all,
Tonight!

(ANITA)

Anita's gonna get her kicks
Tonight.
We'll have our private little mix
Tonight.
He'll walk in hot and tired,
So what?
Don't matter if he's tired,
As long as he's hot
Tonight!

(TONY)

Tonight, tonight
Won't be just any night,
Tonight there will be no morning star.

Tonight, tonight,
I'll see my love tonight.
And for us, stars will stop where they are.

Today
The minutes seem like hours,
The hours go so slowly,
And still the sky is light . . .

Oh moon, grow bright,
And make this endless day endless night!

(RIFF, *to* TONY)

I'm counting on you to be there
Tonight.
When Diesel wins it fair and square
Tonight.

That Puerto Rican punk'll
Go down.
And when he's hollered Uncle
We'll tear up the town
Tonight!

(MARIA)

Tonight, tonight
Won't be just any night . . .

(*She reprises the same chorus* TONY *has just sung.*)

(RIFF)
So I can count on you, boy?

(TONY)
All right.

(RIFF)
We're gonna have us a ball.

(TONY)
All right . . .
(*Regretting his impatience*)
Womb to tomb!

(RIFF)
Sperm to worm!
I'll see you there about eight . . .

(TONY)
Tonight . . .

(BERNARDO *and* SHARKS)
We're gonna rock it tonight!!!

(ANITA)
Tonight . . .
(*All have been singing at once, reprising the choruses they sang before.*)

(BERNARDO *and* SHARKS)
We're gonna jazz it tonight
They're gonna get it tonight—tonight.
They began it—they began it

And we're the ones
To stop 'em once and for all!
The Sharks are gonna have their way,
The Sharks are gonna have their day,
We're gonna rock it tonight—
Tonight!

(ANITA)

Tonight,
Late tonight,
We're gonna mix it tonight.
Anita's gonna have her day,
Anita's gonna have her day,
Bernardo's gonna have his way
Tonight—tonight.
Tonight—this very night,
We're gonna rock it tonight,
Tonight!

(RIFF *and* JETS)

They began it.
They began it.
We'll stop 'em once and for all
The Jets are gonna have their day,
The Jets are gonna have their way,
We're gonna rock it tonight.
Tonight!

(MARIA)

Tonight there will be no morning star.
Tonight, tonight, I'll see my love tonight.
When we kiss, stars will stop where they are.

(TONY *and* MARIA)

Today the minutes seem like hours.
The hours go so slowly,
And still the sky is light.
Oh moon, grow bright,
And make this endless day endless night,
Tonight!

(*The lights build with the music to the climax, and then blackout at the final exultant note.*)

SCENE 9

9:00 P.M. *Under the highway.*

A dead end: rotting plaster-and-brick walls and mesh wire fences. A street lamp.

It is nightfall. The almost-silhouetted gangs come in from separate sides: climbing over the fences or crawling through holes in the walls. There is silence as they fan out on opposite sides of the cleared space. Then BERNARDO *and* DIESEL *remove their jackets, handing them to their seconds:* CHINO *and* RIFF.

BERNARDO

Ready.

CHINO

Ready!

DIESEL

Ready.

RIFF

Ready! Come center and shake hands.

BERNARDO

For what?

RIFF

That's how it's done, buddy boy.

BERNARDO

More gracious living? Look: I don't go for that pretend crap you all go for in this country. Every one of you hates every one of us, and we hate you right back. I don't drink with nobody I hate, I don't shake hands with nobody I hate. Let's get at it.

RIFF

O.K.

BERNARDO

(*Moving toward center*)

Here we go.

(DIESEL *begins to move toward him. There are encouragements called from each side. The "fair fight" is just beginning when there is an interruption.*)

TONY

Hold it!

(*He leaps over a fence and starts toward* BERNARDO.)

RIFF

Get with the gang.

TONY

No.

RIFF

What're you doin'?

BERNARDO

Maybe he has found the guts to fight his own battles.

TONY

(*Smiling*)

It doesn't take guts if you *have* a battle. But we haven't got one, 'Nardo.

(*He extends his hand for* BERNARDO *to shake it.* BERNARDO *knocks the hand away and gives* TONY *a shove that sends him sprawling.*)

BERNARDO

*Ber*nardo.

RIFF

(*Quiet, strong*)

The deal is a fair fight between you and Diesel. (*To* TONY, *who has gotten up*) Get with the gang.

(*During the following,* BERNARDO *flicks* TONY's *shirt, pushes his shoulder, pinches his cheek.*)

BERNARDO

(*To* TONY)

I'll give you a battle, Kiddando.

DIESEL

You've got one.

BERNARDO

I'll take pretty boy on as a warm-up. Afraid, pretty boy? Afraid, chicken? Afraid, gutless?

RIFF

Cut that—

TONY

I don't want to, Bernardo . . .

BERNARDO

I'm sure.

TONY

Bernardo, you've got it wrong.

BERNARDO

Are you chicken?

TONY

You *won't* understand!

BERNARDO

What d'ya say, chicken?

ACTION

Get him, Tony!

BERNARDO

He *is* chicken.

DIESEL

Tony—

A-RAB

Get him!

TONY

Bernardo, *don't.*

BERNARDO

Don't what, pretty little chicken?

RIFF

Tony, don't just stand—

BERNARDO

Yellow-bellied chicken—

RIFF

TONY!

ACTION

Murder him!

SNOWBOY

Kill him!

TONY

DON'T PUSH ME!

BERNARDO

Come on, you yellow-bellied Polack bas—

(*He never finishes, for* RIFF *hauls off and hits him. Immediately, the two gangs alert, and the following action takes on the form of a dance. As* BERNARDO *reels back to his feet, he reaches for his back pocket.* RIFF *reaches for his back pocket, and at the same instant each brings forth a gleaming knife. They jockey for position, feinting, dueling; the two gangs shift position, now and again temporarily obscuring the fighters.* TONY *tries to get between them.*)

RIFF

Hold him!

(DIESEL *and* ACTION *grab* TONY *and hold him back. The fight continues.* RIFF *loses his knife, is passed another by a Jet. At last, he has* BERNARDO *in a position where it seems that he will be able to run him through.* TONY *breaks from* DIESEL *and, crying out, moves to stop* RIFF.)

TONY

Riff, don't! (RIFF *hesitates a moment; the moment is enough for* BERNARDO*—whose hand goes forward with a driving motion, running his knife into* RIFF. TONY *leaps forward to catch* RIFF. *He breaks his fall, then takes the knife from his hand. A free-for-all has broken out as* TONY, RIFF'S *knife in hand, leaps at the triumphant* BERNARDO. *All this happens terribly fast; and* TONY *rams his knife into* BERNARDO. *The free-for-all continues a moment longer. Then there is a sharp police whistle. Everything comes to a dead stop—dead silence. Then a distant police siren: the kids waver, run one way, another, in panic, confusion. As the stage is cleared,* TONY *stands, horrified, over the still bodies of* RIFF *and* BERNARDO. *He bends over* RIFF'S *body; then he rolls* BERNARDO'S *body over—and stares. Then* TONY *raises his voice in an anguished cry*)

MARIA!

(*Another police whistle, closer now, but he doesn't move. From the shadows,* ANYBODYS *appears. She scurries to* TONY *and tugs at his arm. A siren, another whistle, then a searchlight cuts across the playground.* ANYBODYS' *insistent tugging brings* TONY *to the realization of the danger. He crouches, starts to run with her to one escapeway. She reaches it first, goes out—but the searchlight hits it just as he would go through. He stops, runs the other way. He darts here, there, and finally gets away as a distant clock begins to boom.*)

The Curtain Falls

ACT TWO

ACT TWO

Scene I

9:15 P.M. *A bedroom.*

Part of a parlor is also visible. The bedroom has a window opening onto the fire escape, a bed on a wall, a small shrine to the Virgin, and a curtained doorway, rear. There is a door between bedroom and the parlor.

Gay music for CONSUELO, *who is examining herself in the mirror, and for* ROSALIA, *who is on the bed, finishing her nails.*

CONSUELO

This is my last night as a blonde.

ROSALIA

No loss.

CONSUELO

A gain! The fortune teller told Pepe a dark lady was coming into his life.

ROSALIA

So that's why he's not taking you out after the rumble!

(*The music becomes festively, humorously Spanish as* MARIA *enters through the curtained doorway. She is finishing getting very dressed up.*)

MARIA

There is not going to be a rumble.

ROSALIA

Another fortune teller.

CONSUELO

Where is Chino escorting you after the rumble-that-is-not-going-to-be-a-rumble?

MARIA

Chino is escorting me no place.

ROSALIA

She is just dolling up for us. *Gracias, querida.*

MARIA

No, not for you. Can you keep a secret?

CONSUELO

I'm hot for secrets!

MARIA

Tonight is my wedding night!

CONSUELO

The poor thing is out of her mind.

MARIA

I am: crazy!

ROSALIA

She might be at that. She looks somehow different.

MARIA

I do?

ROSALIA

And I think she is up to something tonight.

MARIA

I am?

CONSUELO

"I do?" "I am?" What is going on with you?

(MARIA *sings*)

I feel pretty,
Oh, so pretty,
I feel pretty, and witty and bright,
And I pity
Any girl who isn't me tonight.

I feel charming,
Oh, so charming—
It's alarming how charming I feel,
And so pretty
That I hardly can believe I'm real.

See the pretty girl in that mirror there:
Who can that attractive girl be?
Such a pretty face,
Such a pretty dress,
Such a pretty smile,
Such a pretty me!

I feel stunning
And entrancing—
Feel like running and dancing for joy,
For I'm loved
By a pretty wonderful boy!

(ROSALIA *and* CONSUELO)

Have you met my good friend Maria,
The craziest girl on the block?

You'll know her the minute you see her—
She's the one who is in an advanced state of shock.

She thinks she's in love.
She thinks she's in Spain.
She isn't in love,
She's merely insane.

It must be the heat
Or some rare disease
Or too much to eat,
Or maybe it's fleas.

Keep away from her—
Send for Chino!
This is not the Mar-
Ia we know!

Modest and pure,
Polite and refined,
Well-bred and mature
And out of her mind!

(MARIA)

I feel pretty,
Oh, so pretty,
That the city should give me its key.
A committee
Should be organized to honor me.

I feel dizzy,
I feel sunny,
I feel fizzy and funny and fine,
And so pretty,
Miss America can just resign!

See the pretty girl in that mirror there:

(ROSALIA *and* CONSUELO)

What mirror where?

(MARIA)

Who can that attractive girl be?

(ROSALIA *and* CONSUELO)

Which? What? Where? Whom?

(MARIA)

Such a pretty face,
Such a pretty dress,
Such a pretty smile,
Such a pretty me!

(ALL)

I feel stunning
And entrancing—
Feel like running and dancing for joy,
For I'm loved
By a pretty wonderful boy!

CHINO

(*Offstage*)

Maria!

CONSUELO

It's Chino.

ROSALIA

The happy bridegroom.

CHINO

(*Closer*)

Maria!

MARIA

Please—

CONSUELO

Yes, little bride, we're going.

(*She exits.*)

ROSALIA

They have a quaint old-fashioned custom in this country, Maria: they get married here *before* the wedding night.

(*She follows* CONSUELO *out as* CHINO *enters from offstage. His clothes are dirty and torn from the fight; his face is smeared. They shake their heads at him and flounce out. He closes the outer door.*)

CHINO

Maria? . . .

MARIA

I'm in here. I was just getting ready to—

(*She is hurriedly trying to put a bathrobe over her dress.* CHINO *comes in before she can finish, so that she leaves it over her shoulders, holding it closed with her hand.*)

CHINO

Where are your parents?

MARIA

At the store. If I had known you were— You have been fighting, Chino.

CHINO

Yes. I am sorry.

MARIA

That is not like you.

CHINO

No.

MARIA

Why, Chino?

CHINO

I don't know why. It happened so fast.

MARIA

You must wash up.

CHINO

Maria—

MARIA

You can go in there.

CHINO

In a minute. Maria . . . at the rumble—

MARIA

There was no rumble.

CHINO

There was.

MARIA

You are wrong.

CHINO

No; there was. Nobody meant for it to happen . . .

MARIA

. . . Tell me.

CHINO

It's bad.

MARIA

Very bad?

CHINO

(*Nods*)

You see . . .

(*He moves closer to her, helplessly.*)

MARIA

It will be easier if you say it very fast.

CHINO

(*Nods*)

There was a fight—(*She nods*) And 'Nardo—(*She nods*) And somehow a knife—and 'Nardo and someone—

(*He takes her hand.*)

MARIA

Tony. What happened to Tony? (*The name stops* CHINO. *He drops her hand: the robe opens*) Tell me! (*Crudely,* CHINO *yanks off the robe, revealing that she is dressed to go out*) Chino, is Tony all right?!

CHINO

He killed your brother.

(*He walks into the parlor, slamming the door behind him. A pause.*)

MARIA

You are lying. (CHINO *has started to leave the parlor, but turns back now. Swiftly searching behind furniture, he comes up with an object wrapped in material the same color as Bernardo's shirt. From the bedroom,* MARIA'S *voice calls out, louder*) You are lying, Chino! (*Coldly,* CHINO *unwraps a gun which he puts in his pocket. There is the sound of a police siren at a distance. He goes out. During this,* MARIA *has knelt before the shrine on the wall. She rocks back and forth in prayer, some of it in Spanish, some of it in English*) Make it not be true . . . please make it not be true. . . . I will do anything: make *me* die. . . . Only, please—make it not be true. (*As she prays,* TONY *appears at the fire-escape window and quietly climbs in. His shirt is ripped, half-torn off. He stands still, limp, watching her. Aware that someone is in the room, she stops her prayers. Slowly, her head turns; she looks at him for a long moment. Then, almost in one spring, she is on him, her fists beating his chest*) Killer killer killer killer killer—

(*But her voice breaks with tears, her arms go about him, and she buries her face in his chest, kissing him. She begins to slide down his body. He supports her as, together, they go to the floor, he cradling her body in his arms. He pushes her hair back from her face; kisses her hair, her face, between the words that tumble out.*)

TONY

I tried to stop it; I did try. I don't know how it went wrong. . . . I didn't mean to hurt him; I didn't want to; I didn't know I had. But Riff . . . Riff was like my brother. So when Bernardo killed him—(*She lifts her head*) 'Nardo didn't mean it, either. Oh, I know he didn't! Oh, no. I didn't come to tell you Just for you to forgive me so I could go to the police—

MARIA

No!

TONY

It's easy now—

MARIA

No . . .

TONY

Whatever you want, I'll do—

MARIA

Stay. Stay with me.

TONY

I love you so much.

MARIA

Tighter.

(*Music starts.*)

TONY

We'll be all right. I know it. We're really together now.

MARIA

But it's not us! It's everything around us!

TONY

Then we'll find some place where nothing can get to us; not one of them, not anything. And—

(*He sings*)

I'll take you away, take you far far away out of here,
Far far away till the walls and the streets disappear,
Somewhere there must be a place we can feel we're free,
Somewhere there's got to be some place for you and for me.

(*As he sings, the walls of the apartment begin to move off, and the city walls surrounding them begin to close in on them. Then the apartment itself goes, and the two lovers begin to run, battering against the walls of the city, beginning to break through as chaotic figures of the gangs, of violence, flail around them. But they do break through, and suddenly—they are in a world of space and air and sun. They stop, looking at it, pleased, startled, as boys and girls from both sides come on. And they, too, stop and stare, happy, pleased. Their clothes are soft pastel versions of what they have worn before. They begin to dance, to play: no sides, no hostility now; just joy and pleasure and warmth. More and more join, making a world that* TONY *and* MARIA *want to be in, belong to, share their love with. As they go into the steps of a gentle love dance, a voice is heard singing.*)

(OFFSTAGE VOICE *sings*)
There's a place for us,
Somewhere a place for us.
Peace and quiet and room and air
Wait for us
Somewhere.

There's a time for us,
Someday a time for us,
Time together with time to spare,
Time to learn, time to care
Someday!

Somewhere
We'll find a new way of living,
We'll find a way of forgiving
Somewhere,
Somewhere . . .

There's a place for us,
A time and place for us.

Hold my hand and we're halfway there.
Hold my hand and I'll take you there
Someday,
Somehow,
Somewhere!

(The lovers hold out their hands to each other; the others follow suit: Jets to Sharks; Sharks to Jets. And they form what is almost a procession winding its triumphant way through this would-be world, as they sing the words of the song with wonderment. Then, suddenly, there is a dead stop. The harsh shadows, the fire escapes of the real, tenement world cloud the sky, and the figures of RIFF *and* BERNARDO *slowly walk on. The dream becomes a nightmare: as the city returns, there are brief re-enactments of the knife fight, of the deaths.* MARIA *and* TONY *are once again separated from each other by the violent warring of the two sides.* MARIA *tries to reach* BERNARDO, TONY *tries to stop* RIFF; *the lovers try to reach each other, but they cannot. Chaotic confusion and blackness, after which they find themselves back in the bedroom, clinging to each other desperately. With a blind refusal to face what they know must be, they reassure each other desperately as they sing.)*

(TONY *and* MARIA)

Hold my hand and we're halfway there.
Hold my hand and I'll take you there
Someday,
Somehow,
Somewhere!

(As the lights fade, together they sink back on the bed.)

SCENE 2

10:00 P.M. Another alley.

A fence with loose boards; angles between buildings.

Softly, from behind the fence, the Jet gang whistle. A pause, then the answering whistle, softly, from offstage or around a corner. Now a loose board flips up and BABY JOHN *wriggles through the fence. He whistles again, timidly, and* A-RAB *comes on.*

A-RAB

They get you yet?

BABY JOHN

No. You?

A-RAB

Hell, no.

BABY JOHN

You seen Tony?

A-RAB

Nobody has.

BABY JOHN

Geez . . .

A-RAB

You been home yet?

BABY JOHN

Uh uh.

A-RAB

Me, either.

BABY JOHN

Just hidin' around?

A-RAB

Uh huh.

BABY JOHN

A-rab . . . did you get a look at 'em?

A-RAB

Look at who?

BABY JOHN

Ya know. At the rumble. Riff and Bernardo.
(*Pause.*)

A-RAB

I wish it was yesterday.

BABY JOHN

Wadaya say we run away?

A-RAB

What's a matter? You scared?

BABY JOHN

. . . Yeah.

A-RAB

You cut it out, ya hear? You're only makin' me scared and that scares me! (*Police whistle. He grabs* BABY JOHN) Last thing ever is to let a cop know you're scared or anythin'.

KRUPKE

(*Offstage*)

Hey, you two!

A-RAB

Play it big with the baby blues.

BABY JOHN

(*Scared*)

O.K.

A-RAB

(*Gripping him*)

Big, not scared, big!

(*Again a whistle. Elaborately casual, they start sauntering off as* KRUPKE *appears.*)

KRUPKE

Yeah, you.

(*They stop, so surprised.*)

A-RAB

Why it *is* Officer Krupke, Baby John.

BABY JOHN

(*Quaking*)

Top of the evening, Officer Krupke.

KRUPKE

I'll crack the top of your skulls if you punks don't stop when I whistle.

A-RAB

But we stopped the very moment we heard.

BABY JOHN

We got twenty-twenty hearing.

KRUPKE

You wanna get hauled down to the station house?

BABY JOHN

Indeed not, sir.

KRUPKE

I'll make a little deal. I know you was rumblin' under the highway—

BABY JOHN

We was at the playground, sir.

A-RAB

We like the playground. It keeps us deprived kids off the foul streets.

BABY JOHN

It gives us comradeship—

A-RAB

A place for pleasant pastimes— And for us, born like we was on the hot pavements—

KRUPKE

O.K., wise apples, down to the station house.

BABY JOHN

Which way?

A-RAB

This way! (*He gets down on all fours,* BABY JOHN *pushes* KRUPKE, *so that he tumbles over* A-RAB. BABY JOHN *starts off one way,* A-RAB *the other.* KRUPKE *hesitates, then runs after one of them, blowing his whistle like mad. The moment he is off,* A-RAB *and* BABY JOHN *appear through the fence, followed by the other Jets.*) Look at the brass-ass run!

BABY JOHN

I hope he breaks it!

ACTION

Get the lead out, fat boy!

DIESEL

Easy. He'll come back and drag us down the station house.

ACTION

I already been.

SNOWBOY

We both already been.

A-RAB

What happened?

SNOWBOY

A big fat nuthin'!

A-RAB

How come?

SNOWBOY

Cops believe everythin' they read in the papers.

ACTION

To them we ain't human. We're cruddy juvenile delinquents. So that's what we give 'em.

SNOWBOY

(*Imitating* KRUPKE)

Hey, you!

ACTION

Me, Officer Krupke?

SNOWBOY

Yeah, you! Gimme one good reason for not draggin' ya down the station house, ya punk.

(ACTION *sings*)

Dear kindly Sergeant Krupke,
You gotta understand—
It's just our bringin' upke
That gets us out of hand.
Our mothers all are junkies,
Our fathers all are drunks.

(ALL)

Golly Moses—natcherly we're punks!

Gee, Officer Krupke, we're very upset;
We never had the love that every child oughta get.
We ain't no delinquents,
We're misunderstood.
Deep down inside us there is good!

(ACTION)

There is good!

(ALL)

There is good, there is good,
There is untapped good.
Like inside, the worst of us is good.

(SNOWBOY, *imitating* KRUPKE)
That's a touchin' good story.

(ACTION)
Lemme tell it to the world!

(SNOWBOY *imitating* KRUPKE)
Just tell it to the judge.

(ACTION, *to* DIESEL)
Dear kindly Judge, your Honor,
My parents treat me rough.
With all their marijuana,
They won't give me a puff.
They didn't wanna have me,
But somehow I was had.
Leapin' lizards—that's why I'm so bad!

(DIESEL, *imitating a judge*)
Right!
Officer Krupke, you're really a square;
This boy don't need a judge, he needs a analyst's care!
It's just his neurosis that oughta be curbed—
He's psychologically disturbed!

(ACTION)
I'm disturbed!

(ALL)
We're disturbed, we're disturbed,
We're the most disturbed.
Like we're psychologically disturbed.

DIESEL

(Speaks, still acting part of judge)

Hear ye, Hear ye! In the opinion of this court, this child is depraved on account he ain't had a normal home.

ACTION

Hey, I'm depraved on account I'm deprived!

DIESEL

(As judge)

So take him to a headshrinker.

(ACTION, *to* A-RAB)

My father is a bastard,
My ma's an S.O.B.
My grandpa's always plastered,
My grandma pushes tea.
My sister wears a mustache,
My brother wears a dress.
Goodness gracious, that's why I'm a mess!

(A-RAB, *as psychiatrist*)

Yes!
Officer Krupke, you're really a slob.
This boy don't need a doctor, just a good honest job.
Society's played him a terrible trick,
And sociologically he's sick!

(ACTION)

I am sick!

(ALL)

We are sick, we are sick,
We are sick sick sick,
Like we're sociologically sick!

A-RAB

(*Speaks as psychiatrist*)

In my opinion, this child don't need to have his head shrunk at all. Juvenile delinquency is purely a social disease.

ACTION

Hey, I got a social disease!

A-RAB

(*As psychiatrist*)

So take him to a social worker!

(ACTION *to* BABY JOHN)

Dear kindly social worker,
They say go earn a buck,
Like be a soda jerker,
Which means like be a schmuck.
It's not I'm antisocial,
I'm only antiwork.
Glory Osky, that's why I'm a jerk!

(BABY JOHN *as female social worker*)

Eek!
Officer Krupke, you've done it again.
This boy don't need a job, he needs a year in the pen.
It ain't just a question of misunderstood;
Deep down inside him, he's no good!

(ACTION)

I'm no good!

(ALL)

We're no good, we're no good,
We're no earthly good,
Like the best of us is no damn good!

(DIESEL, *as judge*)
The trouble is he's crazy,

(A-RAB, *as psychiatrist*)
The trouble is he drinks.

(BABY JOHN, *as social worker*)
The trouble is he's lazy.

(DIESEL, *as judge*)
The trouble is he stinks.

(A-RAB, *as psychiatrist*)
The trouble is he's growing.

(BABY JOHN, *as social worker*)
The trouble is he's grown!

(ALL)
Krupke, we got troubles of our own!

Gee, Officer Krupke,
We're down on our knees,
'Cause no one wants a fella with a social disease.
Gee, Officer Krupke,
What are we to do?
Gee, Officer Krupke—
Krup you!

(*At the end of the song,* ANYBODYS *appears over the fence.*)

ANYBODYS

Buddy boys!

ACTION

Ah! Go wear a skirt.

ANYBODYS

I got scabby knees. Listen—

ACTION

(*To the gang*)

Come on, we gotta make sure those PRs know we're on top.

DIESEL

Geez, Action, ain't we had enough?

ANYBODYS

(*Going after them*)

Wotta buncha Old Man Rivers: they don't know nuthin' and they don't say nuthin'.

ACTION

Diesel, the question ain't whether we had enough—

ANYBODYS

The question is: Where's Tony and what party is lookin' for him.

ACTION

What do you know?

ANYBODYS

I know I gotta get a skirt.

(*She starts off, but* DIESEL *stops her.*)

DIESEL

Come on, Anybodys, tell me.

SNOWBOY

Ah, what's that freak know?

ANYBODYS

Plenty. I figgered somebody oughta infiltrate PR territory and spy around. I'm very big with shadows, ya know. I can slip in and out of 'em like wind through a fence.

SNOWBOY

Boy, is she ever makin' the most of it!

ANYBODYS

You bet your fat A, I am!

ACTION

Go on. Wadd'ya hear?

ANYBODYS

I heard Chino tellin' the Sharks somethin' about Tony and Bernardo's sister. And then Chino said, "If it's the last thing I do, I'm going to get Tony."

ACTION

What'd I tell ya? Them PRs won't stop!

SNOWBOY

Easy, Action!

DIESEL

It's bad enough now—

BABY JOHN

Yeah!

ACTION

You forgettin'? Tony came through for us Jets. We gotta find him and protect him from Chino.

A-RAB

Right!

ACTION

O.K. then! Snowboy—cover the river! (SNOWBOY *runs off*) A-rab—get over to Doc's.

BABY JOHN

I'll take the back alleys.

ACTION

Diesel?

DIESEL

I'll cover the park.

ACTION

Good boy!

(*He begins to run off.*)

ANYBODYS

What about me?

ACTION

You? You get a hold of the girls and send 'em out as liaison runners so we'll know who's found Tony where.

ANYBODYS

Right!

(*She starts to run off.*)

ACTION

Hey! (*She stops*) You done good, buddy boy.

ANYBODYS

(She has fallen in love)

Thanks, Daddy-o.

(They both run off.)

The Lights Black Out

Scene 3

11:30 P.M. The bedroom.

The light is, at first, a vague glow on the lovers, who are asleep on the bed. From offstage, faint at first, there is the sound of knocking. It gets louder; TONY *stirs. At a distance a police siren sounds, and the knocking is now very loud.* TONY *bolts upright.* ANITA *comes in from outside and goes to the bedroom door—which is locked—tries the knob.*

ANITA

(Holding back tears)

Maria? . . . Maria? (TONY *is reaching for his shirt when* MARIA *sits up. Quickly, he puts his hand, then his lips, on her lips*) Maria, it's Anita. Why are you locked in?

MARIA

I didn't know it was locked.

ANITA

Open the door. I need you.

(MARIA *reaches for the knob,* TONY *stops her.*)

MARIA

(A whisper)

Now you are afraid, too.

ANITA

What?

MARIA

(*Loud*)

One moment.

TONY

(*Whispering*)

Doc'll help. I'll get money from him. You meet me at his drugstore.

(*In the other room,* ANITA *is aware of voices but unsure of what they are saying.*)

MARIA

At Doc's, yes. (*Aloud*) Coming, Anita!

TONY

(*Kisses her*)

Hurry!

(*He scrambles out the window as* MARIA *hastily puts a bathrobe on over her slip. In the other room* ANITA *has stiffened and moved away from the door. She stands staring at it coldly as* MARIA *prattles to her through the door.*)

MARIA

Did you see Chino? He was here before, but he left so angry I think maybe he . . . (*She opens the door and sees* ANITA's *look. A moment, then* ANITA *pushes her aside: looks at the bed, at the window, then turns accusingly to* MARIA) All right: now you know.

ANITA

(*Savagely*)

And you still don't know: *Tony is one of them!*

(*She sings bitterly*)

A boy like that who'd kill your brother,
Forget that boy and find another!
One of your own kind—
Stick to your own kind!

A boy like that will give you sorrow—
You'll meet another boy tomorrow!
One of your own kind,
Stick to your own kind!

A boy who kills cannot love,
A boy who kills has no heart.
And he's the boy who gets your love
And gets your heart—
Very smart, Maria, very smart!

A boy like that wants one thing only,
And when he's done he'll leave you lonely.
He'll murder your love; he murdered mine.
Just wait and see—
Just wait, Maria,
Just wait and see!

(MARIA *sings*)

Oh no, Anita, no—
Anita, no!
It isn't true, not for me,
It's true for you, not for me,
I hear your words—
And in my head
I know they're smart,
But my heart, Anita,
But my heart
Knows they're wrong

(ANITA *reprises the chorus she has just sung, as* MARIA *continues her song*)

And my heart
Is too strong,
For I belong
To him alone, to him alone,
One thing I know:
I am his,
I don't care what he is.
I don't know why it's so,
I don't want to know.
Oh no, Anita, no—you should know better!
You were in love— or so you said.
You should know better . . .

I have a love, and it's all that I have.
Right or wrong, what else can I do?
I love him; I'm his,
And everything he is
I am, too.
I have a love and it's all that I need,
Right or wrong, and he needs me too.
I love him, we're one;
There's nothing to be done,
Not a thing I can do
But hold him, hold him forever,
Be with him now, tomorrow
And all of my life!

(BOTH)

When love comes so strong,
There is no right or wrong,
Your love is your life!

ANITA

(*Quietly*)

Chino has a gun . . . He is sending the boys out to hunt for Tony—

MARIA

(*Tears off her bathrobe*)

If he hurts Tony— If he touches him—I swear to you, I'll—

ANITA

(*Sharply*)

You'll do what Tony did to Bernardo?

MARIA

I love Tony.

ANITA

I know. I loved Bernardo.

(SCHRANK *comes into the outer room.*)

SCHRANK

Anybody home? (*Goes to bedroom door. Pleasantly*) Sorry to disturb you. Guess you're disturbed enough.

MARIA

(*Gathering her robe*)

Yes. You will excuse me, please. I must go to my brother.

SCHRANK

There are just a coupla questions—

MARIA

Afterwards, please. Later.

SCHRANK

It'll only take a minute.

ANITA

Couldn't you wait until—

SCHRANK

(*Sharply*)

No! (*A smile to* MARIA) You were at the dance at the gym last night.

MARIA

Yes.

SCHRANK

Your brother got in a heavy argument because you danced with the wrong boy.

MARIA

Oh?

SCHRANK

Who was the boy?

MARIA

Excuse me. Anita, my head is worse. Will you go to the drugstore and tell them what I need?

SCHRANK

Don't you keep aspirin around?

MARIA

This is something special. Will you go for me, Anita?

ANITA

(*Hesitates, looks at* MARIA, *then nods*)

Shall I tell him to hold it for you till you come?

MARIA

(*To* SCHRANK)

Will I be long?

SCHRANK

As long as it takes.

MARIA

(*To* ANITA)

Yes. Tell him I will pick it up myself. (ANITA *goes out*) I'm sorry. Now you asked?

SCHRANK

(*As the lights dim*)

I didn't ask, I told you. There was an argument over a boy. Who was that boy?

MARIA

Another from my country.

SCHRANK

And his name?

MARIA

José.

The Lights Are Out

Scene 4

11:40 P.M. The drugstore.

A-RAB *and some of the Jets are there as* ANYBODYS *and other Jets run in.*

ACTION

Where's Tony?

A-RAB

Down in the cellar with Doc.

DIESEL

Ya warn him about Chino?

A-RAB

Doc said he'd tell him.

BABY JOHN

What's he hidin' in the cellar from?

SNOWBOY

Maybe he can't run as fast as you.

ACTION

Cut the frabbajabba.

ANYBODYS

Yeah! The cops'll get hip, if Chino and the PRs don't.

ACTION

Grab some readin' matter; play the juke. Some of ya get outside and if ya see Chino or any PR—

(The shop doorbell tinkles as ANITA *enters. Cold silence, then slowly she comes down to the counter. They all stare at her. A long moment. Someone turns on the juke box; a mambo comes on softly.)*

ANITA

I'd like to see Doc.

ACTION

He ain't here.

ANITA

Where is he?

A-RAB

He's gone to the bank. There was an error in his favor.

ANITA

The banks are closed at night. Where is he?

A-RAB

You know how skinny Doc is. He slipped in through the night-desposit slot.

ANYBODYS

And got stuck halfway in.

ACTION

Which indicates there's no tellin' when he'll be back. *Buenas noches, señorita.*

(ANITA *starts to go toward the cellar door.)*

DIESEL

Where you goin'?

ANITA

Downstairs—to see Doc.

ACTION

Didn't I tell ya he ain't here?

ANITA

I'd like to see for myself.

ACTION

(*Nastily*)

Please.

ANITA

(*Controlling herself*)

. . . Please.

ACTION

Por favor.

ANITA

Will you let me pass?

SNOWBOY

She's too dark to pass.

ANITA

(*Low*)

Don't.

ACTION

Please don't.

SNOWBOY

Por favor.

DIESEL

Non comprende.

A-RAB

Gracias.

BABY JOHN

Di nada.

ANYBODYS

Ai! Mambo! Ai!

ANITA

Listen, you—
(*She controls herself.*)

ACTION

We're listenin'.

ANITA

I've got to give a friend of yours a message. I've got to tell Tony—

DIESEL

He ain't here.

ANITA

I know he is.

ACTION

Who says he is?

A-RAB

Who's the message from?

ANITA

Never mind.

ACTION

Couldn't be from Chino, could it?

ANITA

I want to stop Chino! I want to help!

ANYBODYS

Bernardo's girl wants ta help?

ACTION

Even a greaseball's got feelings.

ANYBODYS

But she wants to help get Tony!

ANITA

No!

ACTION

Not much—Bernardo's tramp!

SNOWBOY

Bernardo's pig!

ACTION

Ya lyin' Spic—!

ANITA

Don't do that!

BABY JOHN

Gold tooth!

DIESEL

Pierced ear!

A-RAB

Garlic mouth!

ACTION

Spic! Lyin' Spic!

(*The taunting breaks out into a wild, savage dance, with epithets hurled at* ANITA, *who is encircled and driven by the whole pack. At the peak, she is shoved so that she falls in a corner.* BABY JOHN *is lifted up high and dropped on her as* DOC *enters from the cellar door and yells.*)

DOC

Stop it! . . . What've you been doing now?

(*Dead silence.* ANITA *gets up and looks at them.*)

ANITA

(*Trying not to cry*)

Bernardo was right . . . If one of you was bleeding in the street, I'd walk by and spit on you.

(*She flicks herself off and makes her way toward the door.*)

ACTION

Don't let her go!

DIESEL

She'll tell Chino that Tony—

(SNOWBOY *grabs her; she shakes loose.*)

ANITA

Let go! (*Facing them*) I'll give you a message for your American buddy! Tell the murderer Maria's *never* going to meet him! Tell him Chino found out and—and shot her! (*She slams out. There is a stunned silence.*)

DOC

What does it take to get through to you? When do you stop? *You make this world lousy!*

ACTION

That's the way we found it, Doc.

DOC

Get out of here!

(*Slowly, they start to file out.*)

The Lights Fade

Scene 5

11:50 P.M. *The cellar.*

Cramped: a box or crate; stairs leading to the drugstore above; a door to the outside.

TONY *is sitting on a crate, whistling "Maria" as* DOC *comes down the stairs, some bills in his hand.*

TONY

Make a big sale?

DOC

No.

TONY

(*Taking the money that* DOC *is holding*)

Thanks. I'll pay you back as soon as I can.

DOC

Forget that.

TONY

I won't; I couldn't. Doc, you know what we're going to do in the country, Maria and me? We're going to have kids and we'll name them all after you, even the girls. Then when you come to visit—

DOC

(*Slapping him*)

Wake up! (*Raging*) Is that the only way to get through to you? Do just what you all do? Bust like a hot-water pipe?

TONY

Doc, what's gotten—

DOC

(*Overriding angrily*)

Why do you live like there's a war on? (*Low*) Why do you kill?

TONY

I told you how it happened, Doc. Maria understands. Why can't you?

DOC

I never had a Maria.

TONY

(*Gently*)

I have, and I'll tell you one thing, Doc. Even if it only lasts from one night to the next, it's worth the world.

DOC

That's all it did last.

TONY

What?

DOC

That was no customer upstairs, just now. That was Anita. (*Pause*) Maria is dead. Chino found out about you and her—and shot her.

(*A brief moment.* TONY *looks at* DOC, *stunned, numb. He shakes his head, as though he cannot believe this.* DOC *holds out his hands to him, but* TONY *backs away, then suddenly turns and runs out the door. As he does, the set flies away and the stage goes dark. In the darkness, we hear* TONY'S *voice.*)

TONY

Chino? *Chino?* Come and get me, too, Chino.

Scene 6

Midnight. The street.

The lights come up to reveal the same set we saw at the beginning of Act One—but it is now jagged with shadows. TONY *stands in the emptiness, calling, whirling around as a figure darts out of the shadows and then runs off again.*

TONY

Chino? . . . COME ON: GET ME, TOO!

ANYBODYS

(*A whisper from the dark*)

Tony . . .

TONY

(*Swings around*)

Who's that?

ANYBODYS

(*Darting on*)

Me: Anybodys.

TONY

Get outa here. HEY, CHINO! COME GET ME, DAMN YOU!

ANYBODYS

What're you doin', Tony?

TONY

I said get outa here! CHINO!

ANYBODYS

Look, maybe if you and me just—

TONY

(*Savagely*)

It's not playing any more! Can't any of you get that?

ANYBODYS

But the gang—

TONY

You're a girl: *be a girl!* Beat it. (*She retreats*) CHINO, I'M CALLING FOR YOU, CHINO! HURRY! IT'S CLEAR NOW. THERE'S NOBODY BUT ME. COME ON! Will you, please. I'm waiting for you. I want you to— (*Suddenly, all the way across the stage from him, a figure steps out of the dark. He stops and peers as light starts to glow on it. He utters an unbelieving whisper*) Maria . . . Maria?

MARIA

Tony . . .

(*As she holds out her arms toward him, another figure appears:* CHINO.)

TONY

MARIA! (*As they run to each other, there is a gun shot.* TONY *stumbles, as though he has tripped.* MARIA *catches him and cradles him in her arms as he falters to the ground. During this* BABY JOHN *and* A-RAB *run on; then* PEPE *and* INDIO *and other Sharks.* CHINO *stands very still, bewildered by the gun dangling from his hand. More Jets and Sharks, some girls run on, and* DOC *comes out to stare with them*) I didn't believe hard enough.

MARIA

Loving is enough.

TONY

Not here. They won't let us be.

MARIA

Then we'll get away.

TONY

Yes, we can. We *will.*

(*He shivers, as though a pain went through him. She holds him closer and begins to sing—without orchestra.*)

(MARIA)

Hold my hand and we're halfway there.
Hold my hand and I'll take you there,
Someday,
Somehow . . .

(*He has started to join in on the second line. She sings harder, as though to urge him back to life, but his voice falters and he barely finishes the line. She sings on, a phrase or two more, then stops, his body quiet in her arms. A moment, and then, as she gently rests* TONY *on the floor, the orchestra finishes the last bars of the song. Lightly, she brushes* TONY's *lips with her fingers. Behind her,* ACTION, *in front of a group of Jets, moves to lead them toward* CHINO. MARIA *speaks, her voice cold, sharp*)

Stay back. (*The shawl she has had around her shoulders slips to the ground as she gets up, walks to* CHINO *and holds out her hand. He hands her the gun. She speaks again, in a flat, hard voice*) How do you fire this gun, Chino? Just by pulling this little trigger? (*She points it at him suddenly; he draws back. She has all of them in front of her now, as she holds the gun out and her voice gets stronger with anger and savage rage*) How many bullets are left, Chino? Enough for you? (*Pointing at another*) And you? (*At* ACTION) All of you? WE ALL KILLED HIM; and my brother and Riff. I, too. I CAN KILL NOW BECAUSE *I* HATE NOW. (*She has been pointing the gun wildly, and they have all been drawing back. Now, again, she holds it straight out at* ACTION) How many can I kill, Chino? How many—and still have one bullet left for me? (*Both hands on the gun, she pushes it forward at* ACTION. *But she cannot fire, and she breaks into tears, hurls the gun away and sinks to the ground.* SCHRANK *walks on, looks around and starts toward* TONY'S *body. Like a madwoman,* MARIA *races to the body and puts her arms around it, all-embracing, protecting, as she cries out*) DON'T YOU TOUCH HIM! (SCHRANK *steps back.* KRUPKE *and* GLAD HAND *have appeared in the shadows behind him.* MARIA *now turns and looks at* CHINO, *holds her hand out to him. Slowly he comes and stands by the body. Now she looks at* ACTION, *holds out her hand to him. He, too, comes forward, with* DIESEL, *to stand by the body.* PEPE *joins* CHINO. *Then* MARIA *leans low over* TONY'S *face. Softly, privately*) Te adoro, Anton.

(*She kisses him gently. Music starts as the two Jets and two Sharks lift up* TONY'S *body and start to carry him out. The others, boys and girls, fall in behind to make a procession, the same procession they made in the dream ballet, as* BABY JOHN *comes forward to pick up* MARIA'S *shawl and put it over her head. She sits quietly, like a woman in mourning, as the music builds, the lights start to come up and the procession makes its way across the stage. At last, she gets up and, despite the tears on her face, lifts her head proudly, and triumphantly turns to follow the others. The adults—*DOC, SCHRANK, KRUPKE, GLAD HAND *—are left bowed, alone, useless.*)

The Curtain Falls

many bullets are left, Chino? Enough for you? (Pointing at another) And you? (At ACTION) All of you? WE ALL KILLED HIM; and my brother and Riff. I, too. I CAN KILL NOW BECAUSE I HATE NOW. (She has been pointing the gun wildly, and they have all been drawing back. Now, again, she holds it out in front of her and turns it on CHINO.) How many can I kill, Chino? How many—and still have one bullet left for me? [illegible]

The Curtain Falls